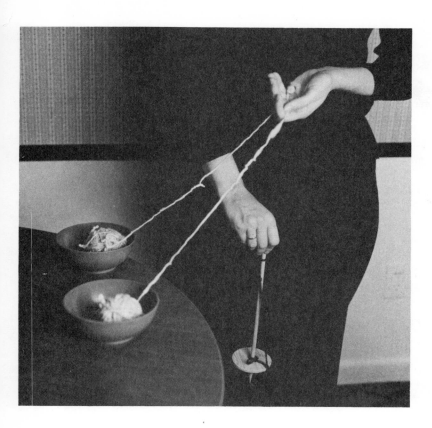

STEP-BY-STEP

SPINNING & DYEING

By Eunice Svinicki

Golden Press · New York
Western Publishing Company, Inc.
Racine, Wisconsin

Crocheted pile rug by Eunice Svinicki. Wool dyed in indigo, cochineal, log-wood chips, and synthetic dyes; cotton backing.

Art Director: Remo Cosentino
Art Assistant: Nora Humphrey
Editor: Caroline Greenberg
Illustrations: Gary Tong
Photography: George Ancona

Library of Congress Catalog Card Number: 74–76679

Contents

INTRODUCTION 4

SPINNING EQUIPMENT 6
  Hand Spindles 6
    The Drop Spindle 6
    The Turkish Spindle 6
    The Navajo Spindle 6
    Making Your Own Spindle 6
  Spinning Wheels 7
    The Castle or Upright Wheel 7
    The Saxony Wheel 7
    The Great Wheel 7
    Parts of the Spinning Wheel: A Glossary . . 8
    The Penguin Quill 9
    Electric Spinners 9
    A New Wheel or an Old One? 10
  Other Equipment 11

FIBERS 12
  Wool 12
    Cleaning 14
    Teasing 14
    Carding 15
    Combing 16
    To Form Roving 16
  Silk 18
  Cotton 19
  Flax 19
    Dressing the Lantern Distaff 20
    Using a Tow Distaff 20
  Miscellaneous Vegetable Fibers 22
  Hair Fibers 22
  Synthetic Fibers 23

SPINNING 24
  Spinning Wool on a Drop Spindle 24
  Spinning Cotton on a Drop Spindle 26
  Spinning on a Navajo Spindle 26
  Spinning on a Turkish Spindle 27

Spinning on a Saxony or Castle Wheel 29
Spinning on the Great Wheel 30
Spinning on the Penguin Quill 31
If You Have Problems 31

YARN DESIGN 32
  Plying Yarn on a Drop Spindle 32
  Plying Yarn on a Spinning Wheel 32
  Worsteds and Woolens 33
  Novelty Yarns 33
  Sizing Yarn 34
  Skein Making 35

DYEING 37
  Preparing the Dyebath 39
  Preparation of Fibers for Dyeing 39
  Mordanting 39
  A Chart of Natural Dyes 40
  Wool, Silk, and Hair Fibers 41
  Cotton, Flax, and Synthetic Fibers 42
  Special Effects and Techniques 42
  Records 45

PROJECTS
  Weaving 48
    Rya Wall Hanging 49
    Woven Table Runner 52
    Woven Weed Holder 55
  Knitting and Crocheting 56
    Knitted Pillow Cover 56
    Crocheted Stole 58
    Crocheted Place Mat 58
  Macramé 61
    Karakul Wall Hanging (Navajo Spun) 61
  Tie-dye and Batik 62
    Tie-dyed Scarf 62
    Batik Scarf 62

BIBLIOGRAPHY AND SUPPLIERS 64

Introduction

Basically, spinning is a simple twisting and pulling technique that produces a single, continuous strand of yarn from a mass of shorter fibers. Twisting the fibers together makes them stronger, while "drawing out," or pulling some of the fibers past each other as they are twisted together, forms a longer strand.

Spinning can be done in a variety of ways, using very simple equipment or the more complex mechanisms employed in factory production. Yarns that have been hand spun may be left their natural color, dyed with synthetic dyes, or dyed with dyestuffs made from native plants.

Early man used the natural fibers that were readily available to him—first, hairlike fibers from reeds and other plants, and later, curly wool from domesticated sheep. The tangled mass of raw fibers was straightened out by using the fingers as a comb; the fibers were then twisted together by hand.

Eventually, man invented the spindle, a tool that could twist, or spin, fibers into yarn more efficiently than his fingers could. The first spindles probably consisted of little more than a grooved stick with some sort of disk, or whorl, attached near the bottom. The whorl acted as a weight to help keep the stick spinning. It also served as a base on which the spun yarn could be wound. Spinners carried their fibers on another stick called a distaff.

When man learned to spin fibers into yarn, and then to weave the yarn into cloth, he also found that he could use natural dyeing substances such as berries, bark, lichens, and roots to color his materials.

The Industrial Revolution brought us the spinning wheel, a tool which greatly reduced human labor by combining the previously separate steps of drawing out fibers, twisting them into yarn, and winding the yarn onto a bobbin. Combs and carders were used instead of fingers to smooth out tangled fibers so they could be spun more easily.

Before long there were spinning wheels fast enough and large enough to spin fibers for mass production. In 1764 James Hargreaves invented the spinning jenny, which could spin more than one thread at a time, and by the end of the century Eli Whitney had invented his famous cotton gin, which prepared cotton for industrial spinning by separating the fibers from the seeds mechanically.

Up until our own century, only natural fibers such as silk, cotton, flax, and wool were used to produce threads and yarns.

fig · 4 ·   fig · 3 ·   fig · 2 ·

Synthetic fibers had been discovered, but it wasn't until after World War I that large-scale production became practical. Though the quality of these man-made fibers was very poor at first, today they closely imitate nature's fibers in many respects. Some that the hand spinner may want to experiment with are discussed in this book.

Along with advances in spinning technology came the discovery of chemical dyes. But while synthetic dyes brought an almost limitless range of brilliant color possibilities to the process of dyeing, natural dyestuffs have continued to yield a more subtle, lovely range of colors with a special beauty all their own.

Today, perhaps as a reaction to mass production and standardization, there is a growing interest in making unique, one-of-a-kind materials. Early man, using simple equipment and natural dyes, produced threads and yarns of great beauty. And so, while technology has provided us with machines and dyes that can give us perfect yarns, many contemporary craftsmen take great pleasure in spinning their own yarns and dyeing them in baths made from natural substances.

This book is intended for all those who enjoy working with texture, fiber, and color—whether in knitting, crochet, weaving, or other crafts—in hopes that it will provide an introduction to the enormously satisfying experience of spinning and dyeing yarns at home.

This eighteenth-century copperplate illustrates spinning with a spindle and distaff (fig. 1), a spinning wheel operated by a foot pedal (fig. 2), winding a skein of yarn (fig. 3), and winding a ball of yarn (fig. 4).

Spindles

drop

Turkish

Navajo

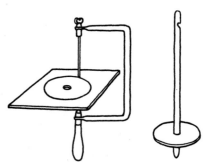

Making Your Own Spindle. To construct a drop spindle for spinning a fine to medium-weight yarn, you will need a 3″ circle of ¼″ plywood and a 12″ length of ¼″ dowel. Drill a ¼″ hole in the center of the plywood circle, slip the dowel into the hole so it extends approx. 2″ beyond the whorl, and glue in place. Sharpen the tip; make a notch approx. 1″ down from the top. Sandpaper all rough edges.

Spinning Equipment

In order to twist fibers into yarn you will need either a hand spindle or a spinning wheel. Since the hand spindle is simpler and less expensive than the spinning wheel, it is a good tool for the beginner. A spinning wheel can be used for greater speed, and electric spinners are available for even faster power spinning. (For how to operate various spindles and wheels, see pages 24–31.)

A few other small pieces of equipment are needed to prepare fibers for spinning and to wind the spun yarn into useable form. Carders, which are similar to a pair of dog brushes, are necessary to straighten out a tangled mass of fibers so that they lie in one direction; umbrella swifts, wrapping reels, and niddy noddys may be used to wind the yarn into skeins after it has been spun. (See Other Equipment on page 11.)

HAND SPINDLES

The advantages of the hand spindle if you are a beginner are many: it requires less speed and dexterity in handling fibers than the spinning wheel; it is easily transported and stored; it is much less expensive to buy than a spinning wheel; and it is a relatively easy tool to make yourself (see diagram). There are several types of hand spindles available.

The drop spindle, which is used primarily for strong fibers such as wool, consists of a tapered rod with a notch at the top. A circular disk or whorl fits onto the rod or shaft. The spinner draws out the fibers, spins the spindle, and allows it to drop toward the floor as more fibers are drawn out and twisted. When the spindle reaches the floor, the spinner winds the spun yarn onto it.

To spin cotton and other weak fibers that cannot support the weight of a dropped spindle, the spindle can be anchored in a bowl, and the fibers twisted upward (see page 26).

The Turkish spindle is quite heavy, with long crosspieces rather than a circular disk to keep it spinning. The crosspieces allow the yarn to be wound into a ball, and then slip apart so that the ball can be removed.

The Navajo spindle was developed by the Navajo Indians. Its shaft is quite long (32 inches); the whorl is approximately 6 inches in diameter. This spindle is rested against the spinner's thigh and rolled down the spinner's leg to twist the fibers into yarn. It is excellent for spinning yarns that are too heavy to be spun on any other type of spindle or wheel.

SPINNING WHEELS

The invention of the spinning wheel unified the previously separate steps of drawing out fibers, twisting them into yarn, and winding the yarn onto a bobbin. The entire process of spinning was made faster and more efficient as a result. In addition, the use of a foot pedal freed both the spinner's hands to work with the fibers, a significant improvement over the hand spindle.

There are several basic types of wheels, each with many variations. Since early spinning wheels were almost entirely handmade, different countries and regions developed their own designs.

Though there are many variations in the design of spinning wheels, your wheel—new or old—will probably approximate the design of the Castle, Saxony, or Great Wheel described below and pictured here and on the following pages. Since a thorough knowledge of your equipment is necessary in order to fully understand the spinning process, it will be helpful to you to study the diagram of the wheel which most closely resembles your own, and to familiarize yourself with the proper terminology for its parts (see the glossary on page 8).

The Castle or Upright Wheel was developed in Europe, and used commonly there. It was compact, yet equipped to handle the same fibers as larger wheels. In the Irish version of the Castle Wheel, the wheel was above the flyer. Another type of Castle Wheel called the Lovers' Wheel had two flyers, which enabled two people to spin at the same time.

The Saxony Wheel was used in America during Colonial times, and is often called the Colonial Wheel for this reason. It could be used to spin any fiber, but was most often used for spinning flax. (See diagram on page 8.)

The Great Wheel was also used in early America. It was sometimes called the Wool Wheel and the Walking Wheel, and was used for spinning wool. It was quite large, and the wheel had to be operated with the right hand rather than through a foot pedal mechanism. The spinner walked away from the wheel to spin fibers and walked toward it to wind the spun yarn onto the spindle. Since the Great Wheel did not accomplish the operations of spinning and winding the yarn onto the bobbin in one process as did the Castle and Saxony wheels, it took more time to operate. Its large size made it somewhat difficult to store. (See diagram on page 9.)

Castle or Upright Wheel

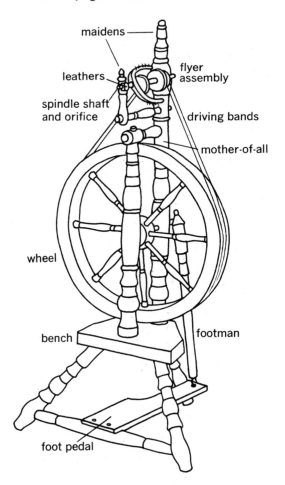

Saxony Wheel

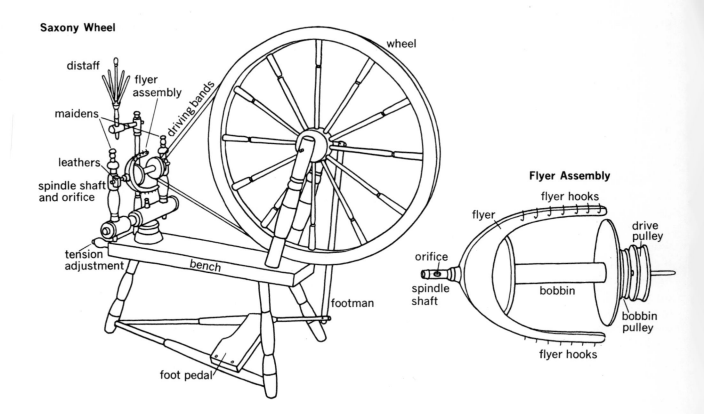

PARTS OF THE SPINNING WHEEL: A GLOSSARY

Bench—the horizontal or slanted plane on which the wheel and the flyer assembly or spinning head rest.

Bobbin—a spool for winding yarn and for holding it for plying.

Bobbin pulley—a pulley on the flyer assembly that revolves at a slower speed than the drive pulley, thus allowing yarn to wind onto the bobbin.

Distaff—a device on some spinning wheels that may be used to hold fibers for spinning. The distaff, when used on a wheel, must be made to fit the wheel. (Two kinds of distaffs are illustrated on page 20.)

Drive pulley—a wooden pulley on the flyer assembly; it drives the wheel and the spindle.

Driving bands—soft cords that run around the wheel and the pulleys as they revolve.

Flyer—a U-shaped apparatus that helps the yarn wind onto the bobbin.

Flyer assembly—the apparatus on Saxony and Castle wheels that actually does the spinning and winding. It consists of the flyer, flyer hooks, bobbin pulley, drive pulley, bobbin, spindle shaft, and orifice.

Flyer hooks—hooks on the flyer through which yarn is guided as it winds onto the bobbin.

Footman—a rod connecting the foot pedal and the wheel.

Foot pedal—the device, operated by the right foot, that sets the wheel in motion.

Leathers—leather attached to the maidens to hold the flyer assembly in place.

Maidens—the posts that hold the flyer assembly.

Mother-of-all—the support for the maidens and the flyer assembly.

Orifice—an opening in the metal spindle shaft of the flyer assembly through which fibers pass for spinning.

Spindle or spindle shaft—the metal or wooden shaft which rotates to spin fibers.

Spinning head—the apparatus on the Great Wheel that actually does the spinning and winding. (See diagrams, page 30.)

Tension adjustment—a wooden screw used to loosen or tighten the driving bands.

Wheel—driven by pulleys, it sets the flyer assembly, spinning head, or spindle in motion. The wheel may be operated by the hand or by a foot pedal.

Wheel supports—wooden posts that hold the wheel upright.

Whorl—a circular disk through which the spindle is held.

Great Wheel

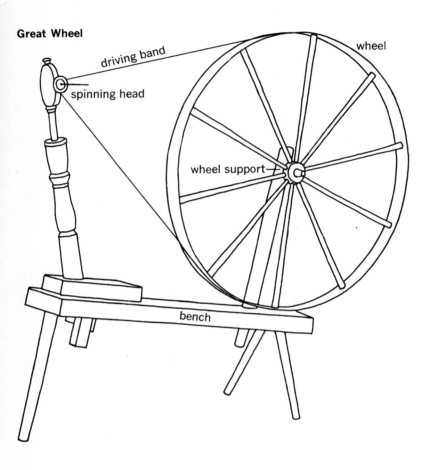

driving band

wheel

spinning head

wheel support

bench

Penguin Quill

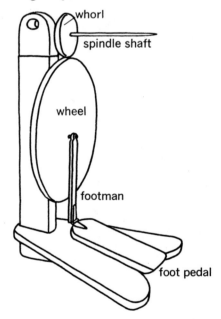

whorl

spindle shaft

wheel

footman

foot pedal

The Penguin Quill. This new design in spinning wheels was created by a University of Colorado engineering professor. It is a compact wheel of modern design which is driven by a foot pedal. The Penguin Quill makes use of a spindle rather than a flyer, and since there is no orifice for the yarn to pass through, there is almost no limit to the size of yarn that can be produced on it. The spinning process is similar to that on the Great Wheel: the spinner draws out the fibers and spins them into yarn while working away from the wheel; the wheel is then reversed slightly to release the yarn from the tip so it can be wound onto the spindle.

Electric spinners have been developed for home use. The electric spinner has a standard spinning head with an adjustable spinning speed. Some spinning heads are available that can be mounted on an old treadle-type sewing machine. This type, though not electric, is excellent for production spinning at home.

A NEW WHEEL OR AN OLD ONE?

Unfortunately, the price of old spinning wheels in America has been driven up by the antique craze in recent years. While genuine collectors' pieces are perhaps getting the prices they deserve, some wheels of poor quality are also fetching high prices. Though it is still possible to find a good spinning wheel for a reasonable price at an auction, it is much less likely than it used to be.

Many people buy old wheels for purely aesthetic reasons, but if you decide to buy an old wheel for spinning, you should be very sure that it can produce yarn. When shopping for an old wheel, look it over carefully, keeping the following points in mind:

1. The wheel should have all its parts. (Those that are most commonly missing are: pulleys, distaffs, flyer hooks, and footmen.)

2. All parts should be in good condition. Look for split, cracked, or broken pieces, and check the foot pedal to make sure that it works.

3. The wheel should not be warped. To check, take the wheel off by removing the wooden pins holding it in place. Check with your eye to see if it is warped. If it is, don't buy the spinning wheel. A warped wheel cannot be repaired easily.

4. The wheel should be in exact alignment with the drive and bobbin pulleys. (On some wheels, the mother-of-all can be moved to accommodate this adjustment.)

5. The ball bearings in the wheel should be in working order. The bearings eliminate friction between moving parts. Treadle the foot pedal to test whether the wheel revolves smoothly. (If it is difficult to treadle, it may only be in need of a little axle grease in the hub.)

6. The grooves in the wheel should not have a glossy finish. (The bands which drive the pulleys will slip on a glossy surface.)

If you know of a good woodworker, broken legs and missing pulleys and spokes can be repaired or replaced. Do not, however, buy a spinning wheel without a flyer assembly or one with a poor wheel. Even if it is a good buy, the repairs may be very costly.

If You Buy an Old Wheel . . .

If you decide to go ahead and purchase an old wheel, you will want to do the following to put it in good working order:

1. Oil the surface of the wood if it's not already finished.

2. Align the bobbin pulley perfectly with the groove(s) in the wheel.

3. To replace the driving bands, cut a length of soft cotton mason cord which is long enough to reach around the bobbin pulley and the wheel, plus 2″. Set the tension screw about halfway. Pull the cord around the bobbin pulley and the wheel. Hold the ends taut and overlap them. Whip the ends together with a strong thread.

Repeat for the drive pulley. (Some spinning wheels have only one driving band running around the wheel from the drive pulley. Another short band runs from the bobbin pulley to a screw mounted on the mother-of-all.)

4. Lubricate all working parts, including the spindle shaft and the inside of the bobbin, with lubricating oil. Place a small drop of oil on the leathers. Lubricate the wheel axle with axle grease.

OTHER EQUIPMENT

Carders are essential for cleaning fibers and placing the fibers parallel to each other. They are wooden brushes with metal teeth set into a leather, vinyl, or canvas backing. Carders can be purchased with fine teeth (about 9 to 10 teeth per inch) or with coarser teeth (5 to 6 teeth per inch).

New carders usually come unfinished; oil the wooden surfaces with linseed oil. If you are purchasing old carders, check for rusty or bent teeth. Rust can be removed by working the carders. The first bits of fiber you card will work off the rust.

Combs are occasionally used by hand spinners to remove all of the short fibers and leave only the long ones. Since retail combs are generally unavailable, the best substitute is a metal dog comb.

Distaffs. These are devices that are sometimes used to hold fibers for spinning. A long distaff can be used to carry fibers while spindle spinning. To spin flax, you will need a lantern distaff or a tow distaff (see page 20).

Drum carder. This is a carding machine which cards the fibers by the turn of the handle. It has metal teeth set into a rotating belt.

Lazy kate. This apparatus is probably familiar to the handweaver. It is simply a rack for holding spools or bobbins of yarn for plying.

Niddy noddy is a comely term used to describe a simple skein maker made of hardwoods.

Threading hooks are simple devices used for threading yarn through the orifice of the flyer assembly on a spinning wheel. The hooks may vary in type, depending on the ingenuity of their maker. A simple hook can be fashioned from a stiff piece of wire with a hook on one end, a spiral on the other, and a piece of ribbon attached to the spiral. Bent paper clips, nails, and crochet hooks are often used as substitutes.

Umbrella swift. This collapsible apparatus attaches to the back of a chair and is used for making skeins of yarn.

Wrapping reel. This is another type of skein maker. The yarn is wound around it into a definite measure.

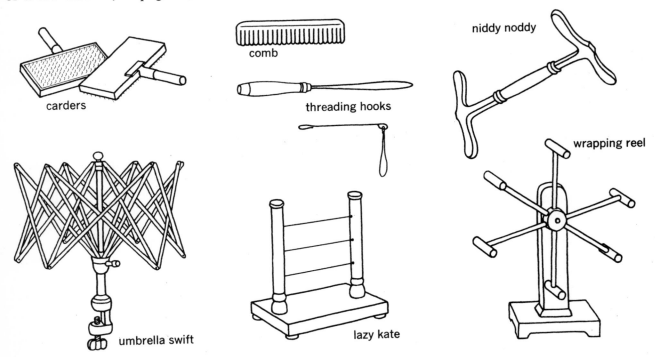

carders

comb

threading hooks

niddy noddy

wrapping reel

umbrella swift

lazy kate

Fibers

A fiber is a hairlike length of raw substance from which yarn is spun. The kind of fiber you choose will depend on the type of equipment you have, what you intend to use the yarn for, and how you plan to dye it. Many interesting fibers are available in various forms through suppliers (see page 64); some you may be able to gather yourself.

Wool, the most commonly used fiber for hand spinning, is also the easiest to spin, and a wise choice for the beginner. Animals such as the alpaca, the llama, the camel, and the goat have coats whose fibers yield unusual yarns. Even your own dog or cat can provide you with a fiber to spin.

Cotton and flax are two common vegetable fibers used for spinning. The East's contribution to the textile world, the silkworm, produces one of the longest and most luxurious natural fibers available. Technology, too, has given us an enormous range of man-made fibers, though they are more often used in machine yarn production than in hand spinning.

Wool

Wool is the soft, curly hair of sheep or lambs; it is sheared annually from live sheep in the spring of the year. Wool varies in quality and color, depending on the breed of sheep it comes from, the region and climate where the sheep are raised, and how well the sheep have been cared for. The major sheep-producing countries are Australia, New Zealand, the British Isles, and the United States.

The climates of New Zealand and Australia are well suited to the Merino sheep grown there. These sheep, raised almost exclusively for their wool, have soft, fine fleeces that spin to a very fine, smooth yarn.

The British raise a variety of breeds, ranging from the goat-like Shetland to the black-faced Suffolks. The Cheviot, Cotswold, Herdwick, Rough Fell, Scottish Blackface, and Swaledale are mountain breeds whose fleece yield a coarse, medium-length wool that is excellent for rug yarn or decorative accessories such as pillows or wall hangings. Longwool sheep, including the Lincoln, Leicester, Devon, South Devon, Teeswater, and Wensleydale breeds, produce long fibers that are also fairly coarse. The wool from such breeds as the Shortwool and Down sheep is shorter and finer, and so more suitable for making wearing apparel.

A Shortwool Dorset raised in the northern United States (photographed at Nine Mile Farm, Menominee, Mich.).

Sheep raised in the United States are classed according to the region from which they come. The Domestic wools, which produce a soft, fine fiber, are found in the eastern and middle western states. The Territory wools come from the Rocky Mountain states. The Southwestern wools come from Texas, New Mexico, Arizona, and southern California. The Rambouillet is a Longwool found in the western United States. It was developed from the Spanish Merino and produces a fine wool similar to Merino wool from Australia. Some medium-length wools produced in the United States are Cheviot and Scottish Blackface. Some Shortwools are Dorset Horn, Hampshire Down, Shropshire, Southdown, and Suffolk.

The karakul, which is relatively scarce, is commonly referred to as a black sheep, although its color may range from brown to shades of gray (see page 16). In common usage, black wool from any source may be referred to as karakul.

The best quality wool from any type of sheep comes from the shoulders and sides of the animal. The back is also quite good. The wool from the belly and legs is usually matted and dirty. Sheep which have been poorly taken care of often have oats, grass, insects, and manure tangled in their wool. The beginner in spinning would be wise to choose a wool that is relatively clean and of medium length, which will produce a fuzzy woolen yarn. A higher quality wool (such as wool from the Merino) will have a longer staple (length) and produce a finer, smoother yarn—but will be more difficult for a beginner to handle.

A high quality wool should possess the following characteristics:

1. high amount of crimp or natural wave
2. low lustre
3. silky feel
4. freedom from foreign matter
5. long staple (length of fiber)

After the wool has been shorn from the sheep, it is called a fleece. A fleece weighs anywhere from 5 to 10 pounds. One pound of wool can yield four 4-ounce skeins of medium-weight yarn, each approximately 200 to 250 yards long. Finer yarns will produce more yardage and heavier yarns will produce much less yardage. (Plied yarns will also produce less yardage than single yarns; see page 32.)

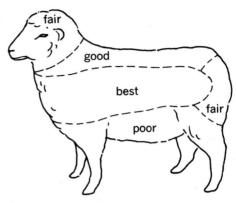

The best to poorest parts of a fleece. (Note: tail area is usually extremely dirty and must be discarded.)

PREPARATION OF FIBERS FOR SPINNING

A fleece which has not been washed is termed "in the grease," because it possesses a certain amount of lanolin. It has an oily feel and a characteristic odor. If the wool is top quality and quite clean, raw fleece can be spun "in the grease" (that is, without washing or scouring it first); it will yield a yarn with water-repellent qualities. The wool must be teased and carded for spinning.

If you purchase a fleece that is dirty, it must be sorted, washed, and carded (see Cleaning, below).

In addition to unwashed fleece, many suppliers sell wool that has been commercially scoured. Often it is sold in roving form (a long, combed, ropelike arrangement of fibers). Roving does not have to be washed or cleaned at home and is ready for spinning. However, since the scouring process removes all the natural lanolin, you will want to spray the wool with olive oil, or perhaps dip your fingers into a bowl of oil while you are spinning.

Cleaning. A whole fleece (sheared from the sheep in one piece) is usually tied together. Untie it and spread it out. Sort the wool according to the chart on page 13. If you can't tell which part of the sheep is which, or if you bought only part of a fleece, sort the wool according to coarseness, crimp, and color. Discard wool that is extremely matted or that is dirty with manure.

Wash the wool, approximately a half pound at a time, in a lukewarm bath of mild soap flakes and water until it is free of dirt.

Rinse the wool thoroughly in lukewarm water. Do not expose the wool to sudden temperature changes, as this weakens the fiber structure. Dry it in the shade; direct sunlight also weakens wool. Do not store unwashed wool which is extremely dirty for a long period of time. Wash, dry, and store it in an open-mesh bag. Add mothballs to the storage bag if you intend to store it for some time. (Wool is an organic fiber and may deteriorate if you do not care for it properly.)

Wool may also be washed in an automatic washing machine. Use the gentle cycle with cold to lukewarm water, and a cold-water woolen wash or a cold-water detergent as the cleansing agent. Adding a fabric softener to the final rinse will make the wool especially soft. Do not use the regular cycle of the automatic washing machine! It will cause the wool to mat horribly and almost spin into yarn.

Teasing. After the wool has dried, pull and tear it apart with your fingers. This helps to untangle the fibers and also allows

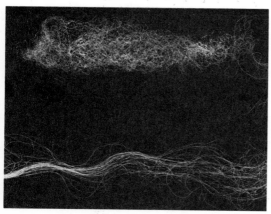

Wool fibers possessing a high amount of crimp

(Top) Down wool of short staple length. (Bottom) Longwool, long staple length.

any hay chaff to fall out. It would be wise to place a newspaper on your lap to catch the fallout.

Carding further cleans the wool and lines it up in one direction. A pair of carders is essential (see page 11). Place a newspaper on your lap to catch foreign matter.

Step-by-Step Carding of Wool

1. Place a handful of wool on the teeth of one carder.
2. Place the other carder on top of the first, with the handles facing in opposite directions and the teeth together.
3. Pull the carders against each other until the wool fibers are parallel to each other.
4. If noils (nubs of short fibers) appear, transfer the wool to the other carder by reversing the direction of the carding (bring handles toward each other). Continue carding as in step 3.
5. To remove wool, pull carders against each other with the handles in the same direction.
6. Roll the wool into long rolls (called rolags) for spinning.

Teasing. Pull the fibers apart with your fingers.

Carding

1. Place wool on one carder.

2. Place the other carder on top of the first.

3. Pull carders against each other.

4. Reverse direction of carding for persistent noils; continue carding.

5. Bring handles together to roll off the wool.

6. Roll carded wool into a rolag.

Range of colors in black sheep

Some Hints for Carding

1. Label carders left and right for the left and right hands.
2. Keep transferring fibers from one carder to the other until all noils or nubs disappear. Otherwise you will have nubby yarn.
3. Card lightly but firmly. Dragging wool through the carders will wear them down.
4. Make up a large quantity of rolags in one sitting to save time.

Combing. If you want a fine, smooth wool, you can comb the fibers to remove noils or short fibers after you have carded it and rolled it into rolags. Use a metal dog comb, and comb the wool as if you were combing tangles from your own hair. (Save the short fibers that build up around the teeth of the comb. You can mix them with other fibers or dye them and use them for tweed yarn.)

To form roving, attach the combed fibers to each other by twisting the ends together between the palms of your hands. To spin with roving, wind it around a distaff (see page 20) or cut it into short lengths approximately 12 to 18 inches long and use directly from your lap.

Step-by-Step Preparation of Wool for Spinning

1. Sort wool fleece.
2. Wash dirty wool in lukewarm water and mild soap.
3. Rinse wool in lukewarm water.
4. Dry wool in the shade.
5. Tease wool.
6. Card wool.
7. Roll wool into rolags
 or
8. Comb wool (optional) and
9. Form roving.

Wool may be combed to remove short fibers.

Form roving from combed fibers by twisting ends together.

"Tree Shadows," rya wall hanging of natural-colored wools by Diane Birkett. A tree branch served as the inspiration for the design executed in natural gray wool.

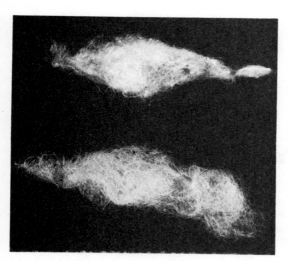

(Top) Wild silk, called tussah. (Bottom) Cultivated silk.

Cultivated silk in bell form

Silk

Silk, whose soft, luxurious feel makes it most desirable for fine cloth, is one of the strongest natural fibers. It comes from the cocoon of the wild worm or the cultivated worm. Wild silk, called tussah, is tan. Cultivated silk is white and of long staple length.

The worm is killed with heat before it has a chance to break its cocoon and complete its life cycle. The cocoon is then softened in water to break down the gum which binds it together. (Silk that is to be dyed must have all the gum boiled off.) A process called reeling unwinds the fiber from the cocoon.

Most spinning suppliers sell silk in roving form which has been combed and is ready to spin. It may also be put up in bell or flake form. A bell is a quantity of carded and combed silk weighing approximately 1 pound. Each bell consists of individual flakes weighing 1 ounce each. The whole bell with its individual flakes actually assumes a bell shape.

PREPARATION OF FIBERS FOR SPINNING

It isn't likely that you will come across a silk cocoon in this country, and even if you did, you shouldn't attempt to unwind or reel the silk from the cocoon. However, you may purchase silk which, though reeled, still needs to be degummed. If the silk you have bought feels gummy, simmer the fibers in a mild soap bath for approximately one hour. Rinse and repeat the bath if necessary.

The silk should then be combed in much the same way as wool (see page 16). Combing removes the short fibers and lines up the longer fibers so they are parallel to each other. The short fibers that fall out during the combing process are termed noils; they are used for a poorer quality silk. (You can save the noils for mixing with other fibers or for spinning a nubby yarn.)

To use a bell of silk for spinning, suspend it near your wheel or spindle. Fibers may be pulled directly from each flake as you spin.

If you buy silk in roving form, wind it around a distaff (see page 20) or cut it into short lengths and use it directly from your lap.

Cotton

Cotton, perhaps the most important vegetable fiber in terms of commercial spinning, is produced in great quantity in the southern United States. It is harvested mechanically, separated into seeds and fibers, and graded according to staple length and condition. Cotton sold by suppliers is already ginned, cleaned, and ready for carding or combing.

PREPARATION OF FIBERS FOR SPINNING

If you live in an area where cotton is grown, you may wish to pick and prepare your own fibers. After you've picked the ripe cotton, pull it from the pod or boll. Then pull the seeds from the cotton.

Since cotton is a relatively clean fiber, no washing is needed. It may be carded and combed, or it may be left as it is for spinning.

Cotton spun without carding or combing produces an irregular, textured, very fuzzy yarn. Fluff or tease the fibers (see page 14) before spinning to make them easier to handle.

Cotton may be carded to free it of any residue of dirt or grass, and to make its fibers lie parallel to one another (see page 15). Carded cotton produces a fairly smooth, slightly fuzzy yarn.

Cotton, ginned and cleaned

Cotton may also be combed (see page 16) to remove the shorter fibers. Cotton that has been carded and combed is very smooth and fine, and produces an even yarn.

Spinning may be done with the fibers held in your lap.

Flax

Flax comes from the woody stalk of the flax plant. A process called retting opens the woody stem enclosing the fibers; running water opens the tissue stem. A process called scrutching removes the pieces of woody stem and is the beginning of the cleaning process. Hackling (which corresponds to the combing process used with other fibers) separates the long fibers from the short fibers and lines the fibers parallel to each other. The long fibers are termed line and the short fibers are termed tow.

Many suppliers sell flax in roving form, already retted, scrutched, and hackled. Flax which has not been prepared in this manner requires a special treatment called dressing before it can be spun. Because flax that has been spun and woven into cloth is called linen, some suppliers sell their fibers as linen rather than flax. They are, however, one and the same fiber.

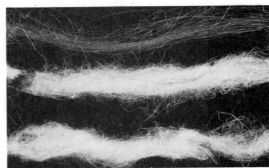

(Top) Coarse, natural-colored flax. (Middle) Fine, natural-colored flax. (Bottom) Fine, bleached flax.

Flax fibers vary in quality and color. A fine flax could be used to spin a cloth for wearing apparel, while a rough-spun flax might be used for toweling. A coarser, natural-colored flax could be used for decorative accessories such as pillows, upholstery fabric, and place mats. Flax can be bleached, dyed, or left its natural brown to tan color.

PREPARATION OF FIBERS FOR SPINNING

The chances that you will use raw flax in this country are slim. But if you do need to prepare your own flax for spinning, first soak the woody stalk in water for several days until it breaks easily (retting). Then beat the outer stalk and the center of the stalk away from the fibers with a wooden paddle (scrutching). Next, hold the bunch of fibers by one end and comb through them with a metal dog comb to remove the short fibers (hackling). After combing, bundle the long line fibers together and dress them on a cone-shaped lantern distaff (see below).

The short tow fibers can be saved and spun also, or mixed with other fibers. Tow fibers and roving should be placed on a tow distaff for spinning.

If you aren't sure whether your flax has been hackled at the factory, shake the fibers out. If they are full of short, coarse fibers, they need to be combed.

Dressing the lantern distaff. Place a cloth or newspaper on your lap. Tie a string to one end of the bunch of line flax. Tie the other end of the string around your waist.

Stretch out the bunch of fibers with your left hand. Begin at the right side. With your right hand, allow a few fibers to fall to your lap.

Work your way back and forth across your lap, allowing a few fibers to drop down evenly. Fibers should form a crisscrossed fan shape as they fall.

When all fibers have been dropped, cut the string from your waist and transfer the cloth or newspaper holding the fibers to a table.

Place the distaff on the right edge of the fibers, with the top of the distaff near the string knot. Cut the knot and loosen the fibers around it. Roll the fibers onto the distaff and put the distaff on the spinning wheel.

Tie the center of approximately 2 yards of ribbon to the top of the distaff. Cross the ends a few times and tie a bow. Pull out the short ends on top to finish. The distaff is now dressed for spinning.

Using a tow distaff. Roving (or short tow fibers) may be wound in and out around the prongs of a tow distaff (see diagram) and the fibers pulled from it as needed for spinning. If you don't have a distaff, you can cut the roving into short lengths, approximately 18 inches long, and spin from your lap.

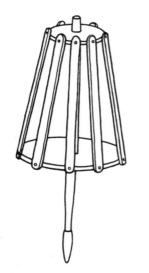

Lantern distaff, for holding line fibers

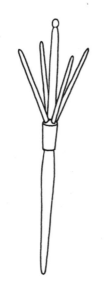

Tow distaff, for holding tow fibers or roving

Dressing the Lantern Distaff

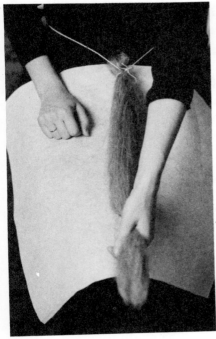

1. Tie the bunch of flax fibers to your waist.

2. Pull fibers away from the bunch, allowing them to fall onto your lap.

3. Work back and forth across your lap until all fibers have dropped.

4. Cut the string from your waist and transfer the fibers to a table.

5. Roll the fibers onto the distaff; return distaff to spinning wheel.

6. Tie a ribbon around the fibers in a crisscross fashion.

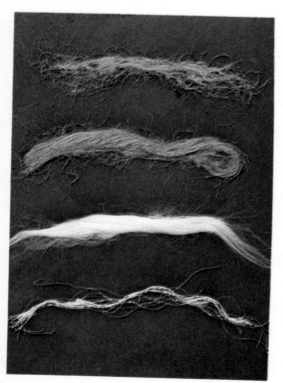

Vegetable fibers (from the top): jute, hemp, ramie, and sisal

Miscellaneous Vegetable Fibers

Jute, grown primarily in India, is a coarse brown fiber which is processed in much the same way as flax. Since it is a weak fiber, it is best spun in a heavy cord or plied from single strands (see page 32).

Hemp is grown in Russia, Poland, and Yugoslavia. It is similar to flax in color and strength, and is usually used to make cordage for fishing lines, net, and roping. It is an interesting fiber to use for wall hangings and other decorative accessories.

Ramie, sometimes called China grass, is often used as a substitute for flax.

Sisal, a vegetable fiber frequently used for making twine, is grown in Africa, India, Mexico, and the Philippines. It is tan in color and has a fairly short staple length. When sisal is spun, fuzzy fibers protrude from the yarn.

PREPARATION OF FIBERS FOR SPINNING

Jute, hemp, ramie, and sisal are often available from suppliers in roving form. If the fibers have not been prepared this way, follow the directions given for dressing flax (see page 20). Again, if you aren't certain whether the fibers have been hackled at the factory, shake the fibers out. If they are full of short, coarse fibers, comb the fibers as shown for combing wool on page 16.

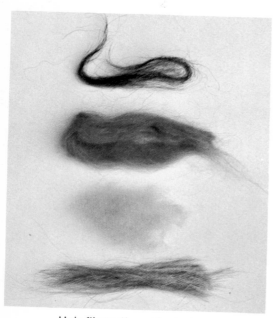

Hair fibers (from the top): yak, alpaca, camel, and horse

Hair Fibers

Many hair-bearing animals produce fibers suitable for spinning. While goat, cow, and horse hair is wiry and coarse, the soft under-hair of some dogs, particularly collies, sheepdogs, and poodles, is especially soft for spinning. Animals related to the domestic dog, such as the fox, wolf, and coyote, produce hair that is suitable for spinning as well.

Members of the camel family produce very soft fibers for spinning. In addition to the camel, with its coarse outer hair and its soft, downy undercoat, the alpaca, the llama, and the vicuna of South America yield excellent yarns.

Several varieties of goat hair, such as mohair, which comes from the angora goat, and cashmere, from the Kashmiri goat of Tibet, are especially good for spinning.

Many interesting and lovely hair fibers are sold by suppliers. But don't forget those that are available at home. Dog or cat hair can be obtained by brushing the animal daily with a wire brush (poodle hair is much easier to spin if the hair is allowed to grow quite long before clipping). You can even save the hair from your own hairbrush—human hair is suitable for spinning, too.

PREPARATION OF FIBERS FOR SPINNING

Prepare most hair fibers much the same way you would wool. Carding is usually unnecessary for cat, dog, horse, cow, or human hair that is obtained from daily brushings (the wire brushes with which the hair is obtained serve as carders). When using tail and mane hair from horses, bundle it together as you would flax.

Any of the hair fibers may be washed in a mild soap bath if they are very dirty. Card and comb them if they are badly tangled.

Spinning may be done with the fibers held in your lap or wound onto a distaff (see page 20).

Synthetic Fibers

The production of man-made fibers has grown by leaps and bounds in recent years. Man-made fibers are classed generically. Each of these groups has several trade or brand names, and not all are suitable for home spinning. Only those synthetic fibers available to the hand spinner will be mentioned here. Generic names are given.

Acetate—a silky fiber often blended with silk, wool, or nylon.

Acrylic—a soft, resilient fiber that washes easily.

Nylon—a strong fiber that blends well with many other fibers and washes well.

Polyester—a fiber that washes and dries easily; it also resists wrinkling.

Rayon—a fiber that imitates linen. It dyes very well.

Most synthetic fibers are manufactured in filament form (see page 32). However, it is not possible to buy synthetic fiber in this form, since most manufacturers chop the long filaments into shorter staple lengths. Some spinning suppliers sell synthetic fibers in roving form.

PREPARATION OF FIBERS FOR SPINNING

Wind roving onto a distaff (see page 20) or cut it into short lengths so that you can spin it from your lap. You can also spin the bats of synthetic quilting material sold in department stores. Fluff and tease up the fibers (see page 14) and spin directly from your lap.

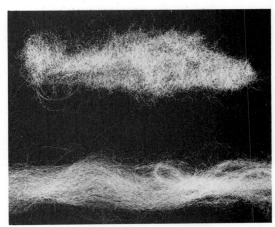

Synthetic fibers: polyester (top) and nylon

1. Tie starter yarn to spindle shaft just above whorl; bring it over the whorl, winding it around bottom of shaft; bring yarn back up to notch. Secure with a half hitch.

2. Stand with carded wool under arm and hold hands at chest height.

Spinning

You can spin on several different types of spindles or spinning wheels, depending on your time, resources, and preferences. The spindle, though it requires more time and patience than a spinning wheel, is a good tool for the beginner. It is also portable and cheap. Power spinners and spinning wheels save time, but require more skill and a larger cash investment than the spindle. The method you choose will depend on which resources are most valuable to you and which method gives you the most pleasing results.

SPINNING WOOL ON A DROP SPINDLE

This type of spindle is excellent for spinning any of the stronger fibers, such as wool, flax, silk, or hair.

Tie a 24-inch piece of spun yarn to the spindle shaft just above the whorl. Wrap the yarn around the shaft a few times. Bring the yarn over the edge of the whorl and wind it around the bottom of the spindle shaft just below the whorl. Bring the yarn up to the notch at the top of the spindle shaft. Make a half hitch loop around the shaft to secure the yarn.

Stand with carded rolags under your arm and hold hands at chest height.

Attach a rolag to the spun yarn by overlapping the ends and twisting them with your fingers.

Draw out fibers from the rolag by grasping them with the thumb and forefinger of your right hand; pull them from your right hand with the thumb and forefinger of your left hand.

Release your left hand only. Twist the spindle to allow the twist to run into the drawn out fibers. Keep hold with your right hand to keep the twist from running up into the rolag.

Continue to draw out fibers. Release your left hand. Twist the spindle in the same direction. Allow the spindle to drop as more fibers are drawn out and the yarn is spun.

When the spindle reaches the floor, undo the loop at the notch of the spindle, wind a few turns around the shaft near the whorl, then wind up and down the spindle shaft so that when it is full it makes a cone. Allow each layer to come a little higher up the shaft. Leave enough unwound to start spinning again.

Continue this process of drawing out fibers, twisting, and winding until the spindle is full. Pull the cone off the spindle carefully and transfer it to another dowel or a knitting needle. Wind the yarn into skeins (see pages 35–36) or balls, or use it directly from the cone.

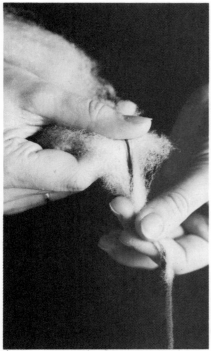

3. Attach starter yarn (dark) to rolag of fibers.

4. Draw out fibers between thumb and forefinger of each hand.

5. Twist spindle with left hand.

6. Allow spindle to drop toward floor.

7. Wind yarn up and down spindle (dark starter yarn is wound first).

8. Repeat steps 3–7 until the spindle is full.

To spin cotton, anchor spindle in a bowl and spin in an upward direction.

Using the Navajo Spindle

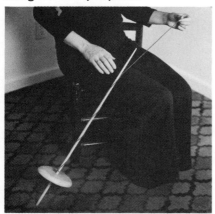

1. Wind starter yarn up spindle shaft and lean spindle against right thigh.

SPINNING COTTON ON A DROP SPINDLE

When spinning cotton, place the spindle in a bowl on the floor or a table—cotton fibers can't support the weight of a dropped spindle. Sit cross-legged or stand; draw, twist, and release in an upward direction. Keep working upward until you can't reach any further comfortably. Wind the yarn onto the spindle as you would with a dropped spindle. This method of spindle spinning can also be used for other weak and short-stapled fibers.

SPINNING ON A NAVAJO SPINDLE

The Navajo spindle is good for spinning extra heavy yarns. Choose a coarse fiber such as wool from a Longwool sheep. (A fine, soft wool is not suitable for a heavy yarn.)

Twist a lead yarn 1½ yards long onto the shaft where it joins the whorl, and then twist it up the shaft. Do not use a knot.

Sit on a chair and lean the spindle against the outside of your right thigh.

Draw out a small amount of fibers from the rolag. Overlap the starter yarn 4 to 5 inches with the drawn out fibers.

Twirl the spindle along your thigh with the palm of your right hand until the twist has traveled into the drawn out fibers.

Draw out fibers between the thumb and forefinger of your right hand, pulling toward the left with the thumb and forefinger of your left hand.

Twirl the spindle along your thigh again until enough twist is in the yarn to hold it together.

Hold the spindle upright by the tip, and turn it to wind the yarn in a crisscross fashion so it will make a cone when the spindle is full.

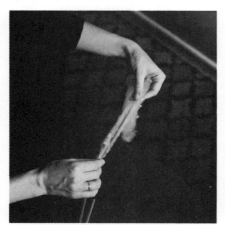

2. Overlap starter yarn with drawn out fibers of rolag.

3. Twirl spindle along your thigh to spin yarn.

4. Wind yarn onto spindle shaft in crisscross fashion.

Repeat the entire process of drawing out, twirling, and winding until the spindle is full. Join new rolags or breaks in the yarn by overlapping the ends and twisting them.

Note: Rolags drawn out to approximately a ¾-inch thickness will facilitate easier spinning.

If your yarn seems lumpy and uneven, try this: after twirling, stop the spinning and hold the spindle firmly in your right hand. With your left hand, pull the rolag to the left until the thicker lumps even out and the yarn is of the desired thickness.

SPINNING ON A TURKISH SPINDLE

The Turkish spindle can be used to spin many different kinds of fibers. It can be used as a drop spindle or anchored in a bowl. Try both methods and decide which is best for you.

Slide the crosspieces onto the spindle shaft and open them to form an X.

Wind a piece of yard-long spun yarn through the wider angles of the X three or four times.

Force the crosspieces open into right angles and make three or four turns through the empty angles of the cross.

Bring the yarn up to the top of the spindle shaft and secure it with a loop (half hitch).

Draw out and spin the fibers as you would with a drop spindle (see page 24).

Wind the spun yarn between the arms of the crosspieces. Follow the pattern made by the lead yarn, varying this path so that the ball of yarn is built up evenly.

To remove the ball of finished yarn, hold it firmly and pull the spindle shaft out of the yarn and the crosspieces; remove the crosspieces.

Using the Turkish Spindle

1. Wind starter yarn through wide angles of X on Turkish spindle.

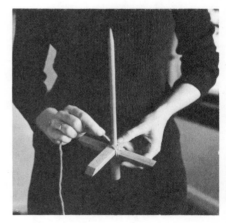

2. Then wind starter yarn through empty angles of the X.

3. Secure with a half hitch at top of shaft; spin as with a drop spindle.

5. Remove ball of spun yarn by pulling out shaft and crosspieces.

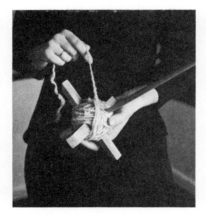

4. Wind spun yarn between arms of crosspieces.

Woven wall hanging by Eunice Svinicki. Driftwood, unspun wool and alpaca, natural-colored linen, and synthetic-dyed yarns were used as filling. Plied cotton was used for the warp.

"Three Beasts," wall hanging by Mary Noonan using fur, seed pods, raffia, unspun and spun wool dyed in onion skins, black walnut hulls, and marigold blossoms.

SPINNING ON A SAXONY OR CASTLE WHEEL

Following is the step-by-step procedure for spinning on a Saxony or Castle wheel, or any other type of wheel with a foot pedal, wheel, and flyer assembly mechanism.

Hold rolags on your lap. Tie an 18-inch piece of spun yarn onto the bobbin, wind it around the bobbin a few times, and hook it through the first hook on the flyer. Using a threading hook, thread yarn through the orifice (the hole in the top of the spindle shaft) so that it extends a few inches from the flyer.

Draw out fibers by holding the end of the rolag with the thumb and forefinger of your right hand and pulling the fibers out with the thumb and forefinger of your left hand.

Twist the end of the drawn out fibers onto the end of the spun yarn with your fingers; overlap a few inches and moisten your fingers to help secure the join.

Depress the foot pedal and treadle it. The wheel may need a push of your hand to start it moving. Start the wheel by the spokes, not the rim, and turn it clockwise for a Z twisting of the fibers and counterclockwise for an S twist (see page 32).

Draw out the fibers; release the fibers in your left hand to allow the twist to spin into the yarn. Keep the wheel moving slowly as you spin. To attach another rolag, overlap the rolag and spun yarn as you did initially.

As the bobbin fills, stop and move the yarn onto the next hook of the flyer. When the bobbin is full, make the yarn into skeins using a niddy noddy, wrapping reel, or umbrella swift (see page 36)—or wind it directly into balls by hand.

If you are using roving, wind it onto a distaff (see page 20) and pull off the fibers from the distaff. Shorter lengths of roving may be spun directly from your lap.

1. Tie starter yarn onto bobbin, catch on first flyer hook, and thread through orifice.

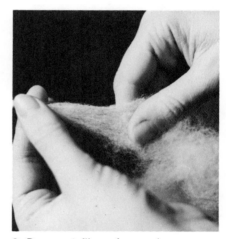

2. Draw out fibers from rolag.

5. Draw out more fibers as yarn winds onto bobbin.

4. Treadle foot pedal and start wheel with your hand.

3. Twist fibers onto end of starter yarn.

1. Draw out fibers while moving away from wheel.

2. Give a slight reverse to wheel; then move forward to wind spun yarn onto spindle.

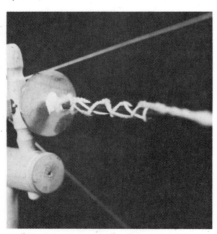

3. Wind spun yarn onto spindle in crisscross fashion.

SPINNING ON THE GREAT WHEEL

The step-by-step directions given here are for spinning on a Great Wheel using a direct drive head. (Instructions for spinning on a wheel using a Minor or geared head follow.)

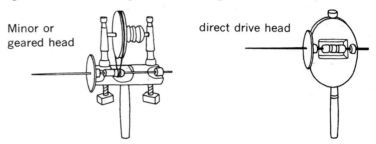

Minor or geared head   direct drive head

The direct drive head is usually found on wheels with a diameter of more than 38 inches. A wheel using this head must be kept revolving slowly and constantly in order to keep the spindle turning. (It is the tip of the spindle that spins the yarn.)

Tie a 24-inch lead yarn onto the end of the spindle; wind a few turns onto the spindle.

Draw out a small amount of fiber from the rolag. Twist the end of the lead yarn onto the end of the drawn out fibers by overlapping a few inches. Rotate the large wheel with your right hand to set the spindle in motion.

Draw out the wool fibers while moving backwards; fibers should snap off the end of the spindle and twist into yarn.

When 50 to 60 inches have been drawn out, give a slight reverse to the wheel, just enough to release the spun yarn from the tip of the spindle. Then continue in the same direction as for spinning. Place the spun yarn against the whorl as yarn winds onto the spindle. Move forward during this operation.

Since the Great Wheel does not have a bobbin or flyer assembly, the yarn is not spun and wound in the same operation. When the spindle is full of yarn, wind the yarn onto a niddy noddy, umbrella swift, or wrapping reel (see page 36)—or directly into balls.

The Minor or geared head is usually found on wheels with a diameter of less than 40 inches. A wheel driven by this kind of head doesn't need to be kept revolving constantly; a half turn of the large wheel will cause the spindle to revolve fifty or sixty times.

To spin with the geared head, follow the directions given for spinning with a direct drive head, except rotate the large wheel with your right hand only a half turn to set the spindle revolving. When using roving, cut it into shorter lengths and place in an easily accessible place while spinning.

SPINNING ON THE PENGUIN QUILL

The principle for operating this wheel is much the same as that of the Great Wheel. You may sit at this wheel and treadle the foot pedal with your right foot. The rolags or roving is held in your lap. Unhook the hook at the back of the wheel. Hook again when not in use to facilitate carrying.

Attach a 24-inch lead yarn to the spindle and wind a few turns around it.

Draw out a small amount of fiber from the rolag and twist it onto the end of the lead yarn.

Set the wheel in motion by treadling with your right foot. The wheel may need a slight push to start it moving.

Draw out fibers by holding the end of the rolag with the thumb and forefinger of your right hand and pulling the fibers out with the thumb and forefinger of your left hand.

Release hold of the fibers with your left hand to allow the twist to spin into the drawn out fibers; keep the wheel slowly revolving. Continue to draw out and release fibers for twisting until the length is too long to work with comfortably. Give a slight reverse to the wheel, just enough to release the yarn from the tip. Then continue treadling to wind yarn onto the spindle.

IF YOU HAVE PROBLEMS . . .

1. If your yarn won't feed in, the problem could be:
  a. the yarn is too thick to pass through the orifice
  b. the yarn is caught on the flyer hook
  c. the yarn isn't hooked on the flyer hook and is wrapping around the spindle shaft
  d. the tension on the driving bands is too slack. In this case, tighten the screw.
2. If the wheel reverses direction, practice treadling without spinning any yarn.
3. If yarn breaks or fibers pull apart before twisting, stop and overlap the fibers to twist them back together with your fingers. Two spun yarns can't be joined very easily, but a new start of fibers can be joined to a broken spun yarn.
4. If the whole rolag starts to feed in before you have it drawn out, stop and draw out the fibers; then spin. It will take practice to learn to draw out the fibers and spin continually.
5. If your yarn is kinky, it is overspun. Slow down your treadling, slacken tension so that the yarn feeds in faster, or hold back on the fibers to maintain tension as the fibers are being spun.
6. If your yarn is lumpy, card the fibers better and draw them out to an even thickness.

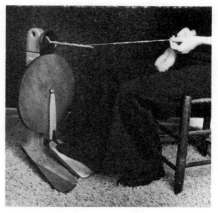

1. Spin fibers off the spindle tip while treadling foot pedal.

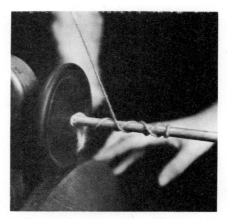

2. Give a slight reverse to the wheel to release yarn; wind yarn in crisscross fashion up the spindle shaft.

3. Wind yarn back down spindle shaft and continue spinning.

Z twist   S twist

Plying yarn on a drop spindle

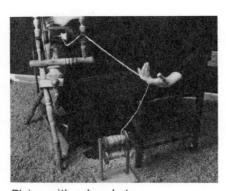

Plying with a lazy kate

Plying without a lazy kate

Yarn Design

In yarn design, fibers are classified as either staple fibers or filament fibers. **Staple fibers** are short enough to be measured in inches; **filament fibers** are measured in yards. Staple fibers come from all the natural fibers except some kinds of silk. (Some silk is long enough to be measured in yards, and so is termed filament silk.) Most man-made fibers are produced in filament form and then cut into shorter staple lengths. Staple fibers require much more twist than do filament fibers.

A single is a strand of fibers twisted together. A single twisted in a clockwise direction is called a Z twist. A single twisted in a counterclockwise direction is called an S twist. The direction in which you turn your wheel or spindle determines the direction of the twist.

Ply yarn is composed of two or more singles twisted together. The singles are twisted in the opposite direction to which they were spun. Two-ply yarn is composed of two singles, three-ply yarn of three singles, and so on.

A cord consists of two or more plied yarns that are twisted together in another operation.

PLYING YARN ON A DROP SPINDLE

Tie a lead yarn onto the spindle as for spinning singles.

Place two balls of spun yarn in bowls. Tie the ends of each ball to the lead yarn.

Place singles between the fingers of your left hand as shown and twist the spindle with your right hand. Twist the spindle in the direction opposite to which the singles were spun.

PLYING YARN ON A SPINNING WHEEL

With a lazy kate. Place the appropriate number of bobbins (one for each ply) on a lazy kate bobbin holder.

Place singles between the fingers of your left hand; attach singles to the lead yarn by twisting with your fingers.

Rotate the wheel in the opposite direction to which the yarn was spun originally; allow the yarn to spin through.

Without a lazy kate. Place one ball of yarn for each ply in bowls.

Attach singles to the lead yarn by overlapping the ends and twisting them together with your fingers. For two-ply, singles may be held as shown; for three-ply or more, place singles between the fingers of your left hand.

Spin yarn through in the opposite direction to which the original singles were spun.

WORSTEDS AND WOOLENS

A worsted is a smooth, strong yarn that has been spun from a medium to long staple wool. Use carded and combed fibers, and allow a good deal of twist to develop. (Take care not to overtwist, however, or the yarn will be kinky in places.)

A woolen is a soft, fuzzy yarn, slightly heavier than a worsted, that is particularly suitable for short staple fibers that have been carded. It is spun with just enough twist to hold it together.

NOVELTY YARNS

Novelty yarns often consist of a base yarn with another yarn twisted around it for a textured effect, although singles can also be altered in various ways to create unusual interest. Manufacturers make many types of novelty yarns; a few that can be hand spun are described here.

Bouclé. This yarn is characterized by tight loops projecting from the yarn at regular intervals. Spin two singles, one medium and one fine. Ply yarn into a bouclé by twisting the medium yarn into loops at regular intervals with the thumb and index finger of your right hand. The fine yarn acts as a tie to hold the loops in place. Ply in the opposite direction to which the singles were spun. (Note that the loops are closed in hand-spun bouclé.) Another way to make bouclé is to hold one single between the thumb and index finger of each hand. At regular intervals, slacken the tension on one single and allow it to snarl up. Hold the other single taut.

Cord yarns. A cord is used as the base here, with a carded fiber loosely spun around it. This type of yarn is usually heavy, and provides an interesting textural effect in macramé and woven wall hangings.

Corkscrew yarns. There are two types of corkscrew yarn you can make: **1.** Spin two regular singles. Ply by holding one single between the thumb and index finger of one hand and the other single in the other hand. Hold one single taut and the other more loosely. The loose single will corkscrew around the taut one. **2.** Ply two different thicknesses of yarn together. The heavier yarn will wrap around the finer one.

Slub yarn. Soft untwisted spots appear at frequent intervals in this yarn. Spin a single yarn; at various intervals, allow a "slub" of yarn to pass through your fingers without twisting. (Poorly carded wool will easily produce a slub yarn.)

Spot yarn. Spot yarn is characterized by a spot of effect yarn showing up at regular intervals. Spin a single yarn; at various intervals, add a spot of another fiber or color. Spots may be

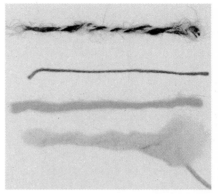

(From the top) Two-color plied tweed, worsted, woolen, and cord yarns

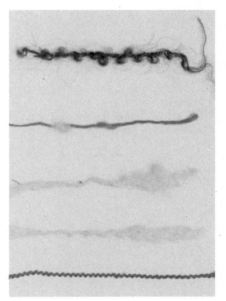

(From the top) Bouclé, tweed or spot, slub, thick and thin, and corkscrew yarns

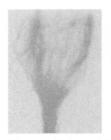
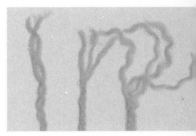

(From left to right) A single; two-ply, three-ply, and four-ply yarns

Stitchery plaques by Glenna Gray using homespun yarns dyed in natural dyes. The bottom plaque incorporates batik elements as part of the design.

saved from the noils left from carding. If the spots are quite small and of various colors, the yarn becomes a tweed.

Thick and thin yarn. This is a single yarn with thick twisted places and thin twisted places. Spin a single yarn and allow alternate thicknesses of fibers to pass through your fingers.

Tweeds. To spin a spot tweed, spin colored spots into a base fiber. Keep the spots of colored fibers in a small bowl next to you. At close intervals, pick up a spot with moistened fingers and drop it into the fibers as they are drawn out and spun. (Save the noils from carding to use as spots.) To spin a plied tweed, ply two or more colors of yarn together.

Yarn mixtures. Yarns may be made by mixing various colors or fibers. Cotton and linen are common fiber mixtures. The synthetics are often mixed with cotton or wool. Fibers or yarns may be mixed by: **1.** Carding. Place small amounts of two or more colors or fibers on carders and card to mix. Spin as usual. **2.** Plying. Ply two or more colors or fibers together.

SIZING YARN

After you have gained some experience in spinning and have begun to produce consistent yarns, you will want to know how to classify your yarn according to yardage and thickness. A system of counting used in the machine spinning of wool, cotton, silk, and synthetics can be applied here as a guide.

The count of yarn is determined by the number of skeins of a given yardage it takes to produce 1 pound of yarn. The following is a list of common counts. To find the count of your yarn, decide how many skeins you must make to produce skeins of the yardage given for the various fibers. For example, if 560 yards of worsted wool weighs 1 pound, the count of that yarn is #1. If it takes two 560-yard skeins to make up a pound, the count of that yarn is #2. Higher counts indicate finer yarns.

Cotton count = the number of 840-yard skeins that make up 1 pound.

Woolen count = the number of 1600-yard skeins that make up 1 pound.

Worsted count = the number of 560-yard skeins that make up 1 pound.

Spun silk = the number of 840-yard skeins needed to make up 1 pound.

Linen = the number of yards weighing 1 pound divided by 300 yards.

To find the yardage of plied yarn, divide the ply number into the yarn number and multiply by the yardage given for singles.

Skein Making

If you plan to ply your yarn, it may be left on the bobbins or wound into balls. Yarn that is to be used "au naturel" (without dyeing) for knitting or crocheting can also be wound directly into balls. It isn't necessary to remove the bobbin from a Saxony or Castle wheel when winding yarn. Yarn from a spindle can be removed in cone form and a knitting needle or dowel inserted into the cone for winding, or the yarn may be wound directly from the spindle.

However, if you intend to dye your yarn, you will want to make it into skeins.

Skeining by hand. Hold your arm and hand in the bent position shown. Starting at the base of your thumb, begin winding the yarn from thumb to elbow and back to your thumb. Remove the yarn, twist the ends together, and tie loosely.

Making Skeins by Hand

1. Wind yarn from base of thumb to elbow and back again.

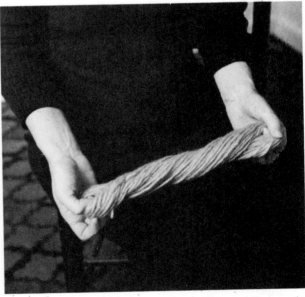

2. Remove yarn, twist the ends together, and tie loosely.

Using a niddy noddy. Tie the end of the yarn onto one of the notched ends of the niddy noddy. Wind the yarn in two V shapes as shown (a complete revolution measures 2 yards). Slip the yarn off the unnotched end of the niddy noddy after you have wound a full skein.

Hold the skein on your hands as shown and twist it several times. Tie each end loosely.

Remove your hand from one end and bring the ends together. Twist the skein again and tie it loosely.

Using an umbrella swift. Clamp the umbrella swift onto a table or the back of a chair and spread it into a definite measure, such as 1½ or 2 yards. (Use a tape measure to determine the circumference.) Tie the end of the yarn onto the swift. Wind the yarn around the swift until you have a full skein. Keep track of the number of winds, so you know the exact yardage. Collapse the swift slightly, untie the yarn, and remove it from the swift. Finish the skein as described in using a niddy noddy.

Using a wrapping reel. Tie an end of the yarn onto one of the spokes. Guide the yarn around the reel. When the reel is full, remove the yarn and finish the skein as described in using a niddy noddy.

Using a Niddy Noddy

1. After winding a full skein (see photo on the right), slip yarn off niddy noddy; hold ends of skein over hands and twist several times.

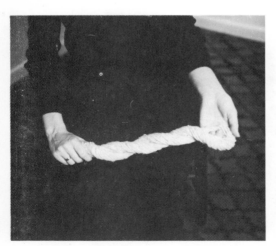

2. Bring ends together and twist again. Tie loosely.

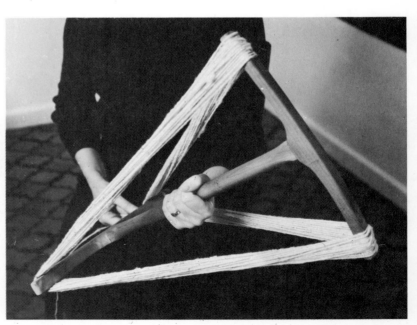

(Above) Tie yarn onto one of the notched ends of the niddy noddy and wind yarn in two V shapes. Wind a full skein.

Dyeing

When man learned to spin fibers into yarn and weave the yarn into cloth, he also learned that certain substances could be used to dye his cloth. Before the advances of technology, man relied on natural dyeing substances such as berries, bark, lichens, and roots. Later, the discovery of chemical dyes brought a brilliant range of colors to the process of dyeing.

Yarns that have been hand spun may be left their natural color, dyed with synthetic dyes, or dyed with natural dyes.

Synthetic or chemical dyes are produced by mixing certain chemicals of a salt or acid base. Synthetic dyes provide an almost limitless range of colors, and several types are available to consumers (specific directions are given on each package).

Natural dyes, which may be made from various plants and insects, provide a more subtle range of colors which are lovely in themselves. A mordant or chemical salt must be used with most natural dyes to fix the color. You can purchase natural dyestuffs through suppliers (see page 64), or you can gather them yourself.

Cochineal, which yields a red dye, is an insect that feeds on the cactus plant. A tiny snail produces a purple dye. Indigo, which comes from a flowering plant, yields a blue dye. Logwood chips, taken from the bark of the logwood tree, give a black to purple dye.

Many other beautiful colors can be obtained from dyestuffs found in the kitchen, woods, or garden. The garden yields gold from marigolds, pink from red beets, and green from grasses. Brown dye can be obtained from coffee or tea, purple from blueberries or grape juice, pink from cranberries, and orange from onion skins. The woods and fields yield an abundance of yellow, gold, tan, and gray dyes. Sumac berries produce a tan dye, maple bark gives us a gray, goldenrod produces yellow dye, and mosses and lichens give us green dye.

The availability of various plants that are sources of natural dyestuffs will vary from area to area, depending on soil conditions, rainfall, and length of growing season. Dyestuffs such as berries and blossoms should be picked at the height of their growing season. They may then be used fresh, dried, canned, or frozen. (If you are drying dyestuffs, be sure to store them in a cool, dry place; moldy dyestuffs will affect color adversely. Once a dyestuff has been made into a liquid dye, it can be canned or frozen for future use.)

If you are experimenting with various plants in your locality and are uncertain whether or not they can be used for dyeing,

Woven purse with willow handles and cork closures, by S. Dorsheimer. Handspun wool dyed in synthetic dyes.

Color Wheel of Natural Dyes

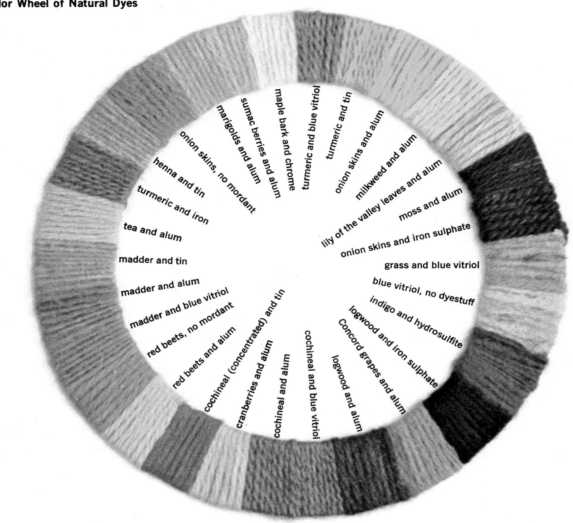

Labels around the wheel (clockwise from top):

maple bark and blue vitriol
turmeric and tin
onion skins and alum
milkweed and alum
lily of the valley leaves and alum
moss and alum
onion skins and iron sulphate
grass and blue vitriol
blue vitriol, no dyestuff
indigo and hydrosulfite
logwood and iron sulphate
Concord grapes and alum
logwood and alum
cochineal and blue vitriol
cochineal and alum
cochineal (concentrated) and tin
cranberries and alum
red beets and alum
red beets, no mordant
madder and blue vitriol
madder and alum
madder and tin
tea and alum
turmeric and iron
henna and tin
onion skins, no mordant
marigolds and alum
sumac berries and alum
maple bark and chrome
turmeric and blue vitriol

Neutral colors (from the left): logwood chips and iron sulphate, black walnut hulls and alum, henna and alum, maple bark and iron sulphate, horse chestnuts and iron sulphate, sumac berries and iron sulphate, coffee and chrome

---

Effect of Mordants on Color

Cochineal with: alum, chrome, tin, (concentrated cochineal), and iron sulphate

Onion skins with: alum, chrome, tin, no mordant, and iron sulphate

Logwood with: alum, copper sulphate, chrome, iron sulphate, iron sulphate (concentrated logwood)

crush the substance between your fingers; if it leaves a stain it might be a potential dye. Sometimes, however, the color of the blossom or berry is not the color of the resulting dye, so it is a good idea when experimenting to produce a small amount of dye for testing purposes.

The equipment needed for dyeing is quite simple: large enamel pots (with covers), glass rods (for stirring), rubber gloves, cheese-cloth, a scale, and a heating unit.

PREPARING THE DYEBATH

A good rule of thumb to follow in determining amounts of dyestuffs is to use 1 pound of fresh dyestuff to dye 1 pound of fiber. To prepare the dyestuff and dyebath, follow these instructions.

Step-by-Step Preparation of Dyebath

1. Gather 1 pound of dyestuff for each pound of fiber to be dyed. Pick out all foreign matter and dirt.
2. Place dyestuff in an enamel container and barely cover with soft water. Steep in water overnight.
3. Pulverize dyestuff to bring out the dye pigments. You can use a blender for dyestuffs such as grass, beets, or berries. Harder dyestuffs such as bark and nuts should be broken or pounded into small pieces.
4. Bring the water and dyestuff to a boil in enamel container. Simmer, covered, for one hour.
5. Strain off the liquid through a cheesecloth.
6. Add 4 gallons of soft water to the strained dye concentrate.

Now you must prepare your fiber for dyeing, and select the proper mordant (see Mordanting, below).

PREPARATION OF FIBERS FOR DYEING

Fibers may be dyed before spinning or after they have been made into yarn. If you are dyeing spun yarn, tie it into loose skeins (see pages 35–36). Do not tie it too tightly or rings will appear where the dye is unable to penetrate.

Wetting. Always wet your fiber or yarn in a mild soap bath prior to dyeing. Wetting will prevent spotting and uneven color. Never place dry fiber directly into a mordant bath (see below) or a dyebath.

MORDANTING

Mordants are chemical salts which affect the color fastness and permanency of natural dyes. The mordant attaches itself to the fiber and the dye attaches itself to the mordant. Almost all vegetable dyes require a mordant, although some plants contain mordants within their composition and so do not re-

A CHART OF NATURAL DYES

Dyestuff	Mordant	Color
Beets, red	alum	pink
Beets, red	none	rose pink
Black walnut hulls	iron sulphate	gray
Birch bark	alum	tan
Birch, white, leaves	alum	yellow
Bracken fern	blue vitriol	green
Cochineal	alum	rose-red
Cochineal	chrome	red-purple
Cochineal	iron sulphate	blue-purple
Cochineal (concentrated)	tin	bright red
Coffee	alum	light brown
Cranberries	alum	pink
Cutch	alum	brown
Fustic chips	alum	blue
Goldenrod blossom	alum	yellow
Grapes, Concord	alum	purple
Grass	blue vitriol	green
Henna	alum or iron	brown
Horse chestnut	alum	brown
Indigo	hydrosulfite	blue
Lichens	alum	light olive-green
Lichens	tin	orange
Lily of the valley leaves	alum	green
Logwood chips	alum	purple
Logwood chips	iron sulphate	navy blue
Logwood chips (concentrated)	iron sulphate	black
Madder	alum	orange-red
Madder	tin	orange
Maple bark	alum	tan
Maple bark	iron sulphate	gray
Marigold blossoms	alum	light gold
Marigold blossoms	chrome	deep gold
Milkweed blossoms	alum	yellow
Moss	iron sulphate	olive-green
Onion skins	none	orange
Onion skins, dried	chrome	bright gold
Onion skins, dried	iron sulphate	olive-green
Peach leaves	alum	yellow
Sandalwood, red	alum	brown
Sumac berries	alum	tan
Sumac berries	iron sulphate	gray
Tea	alum	shrimp

quire one. Wool, silk, and hair fibers require different mordants than do the vegetable fibers (see below). Mordants have a certain amount of color in themselves, and so they will affect the color of the resulting dye.

Water, which sometimes contains a small amount of mordant, can also affect the dye. (Many waters contain iron, which is a chemical salt.) Soft water is recommended for dyeing. Hard water may be softened by adding acetic acid (vinegar) or a commercial product.

Mordants listed in dye recipes are often termed by common names, but it is wise to learn the chemical names of commonly used mordants. Chemists and chemical suppliers know and sell their products by these names.

Common Names of Mordants	Chemical Names of Mordants
Alum	potassium aluminum sulfate
Blue vitriol	cupric sulfate
Chrome	potassium dichromate
Iron or iron sulphate	ferrous sulfate
Tin	stannous chloride

Common Household Products Used as Mordants
Alum—ammonium type for pickling
Lye—caustic soda
Salt—sodium chloride
Washing soda—sodium carbonate

Since mordants do affect color, use a mordant in a color range that is close to the color of the dye. Using a mordant in a different color range may change the color of the dye completely. For example, dried onion skins with a chrome mordant yield gold, but onion skins with iron sulphate yield olive-green. The color range of various mordants follows:

Mordant	For Ranges of
Alum	yellow, yellow-green
Blue vitriol	green
Chrome	gold, red
Iron sulphate	gray, black, olive-green, purple
Tin	gold, orange, red

WOOL, SILK, AND HAIR FIBERS

Adding mordant to dyebath. For 1 pound of wool, silk, or the hair fibers, dissolve the specified amount of mordant (see page 42) in 4 gallons of dyebath before adding the wetted fiber.

Pre-mordanting the fiber. For 1 pound of wool, silk, or hair fibers, dissolve the specified amount of mordant in 4 gallons of soft water. Add wetted fiber and simmer for one hour. Then place the mordanted fiber in the dyebath.

Mordant	Amounts to Use
Alum	3 to 4 ounces per pound of fiber
Blue vitriol	3 to 4 ounces per pound of fiber
Chrome	½ ounce per pound of fiber
Iron sulphate	½ ounce per pound of fiber
Tin	½ ounce per pound of fiber

COTTON, FLAX, AND SYNTHETIC FIBERS

Cotton dyes fairly well with proper mordanting, but flax and similar vegetable fibers such as hemp do not accept dyeing readily. Synthetic fibers, with the exception of rayon, do not take dyes easily either. Whereas wool, silk, and the hair fibers can be mordanted in any of the mordants listed above, the vegetable and synthetic fibers should be mordanted as follows:

Prepare a solution of 1 ounce of cream of tartar and 4 ounces of alum to 4 gallons of water. Add the wetted fiber and simmer for one hour.

Step-by-Step Procedure for Dyeing All Fibers
1. Gather dyestuff.
2. Steep overnight in just enough water to cover.
3. Pulverize (in a blender, if possible).
4. Bring to a boil, then simmer for one hour.
5. Strain off liquid through cheesecloth.
6. For each pound of dyestuff gathered, add 4 gallons soft water to dye concentrate.
7. Tie spun fiber in loose skeins (or dye before spinning).
8. Pre-mordant fiber before dyeing, or add mordant to dyebath.
9. Add wetted fiber to dyebath.
10. Simmer for approximately one hour, or until fiber is a shade darker than desired. Stir occasionally with a glass rod.
11. Remove fiber from dyebath with rubber gloves.
12. Rinse in successively cooler baths until water runs clear.
13. Squeeze out excess water; do not wring.
14. Dry away from direct heat or sunlight.

SPECIAL EFFECTS AND TECHNIQUES

Dyeing can be done by the fiber, the yarn, or the finished piece. Color permanency is greatest in fiber dyeing, while dyeing yarn allows for more variations in fabricating the final project. Dyeing the woven, knitted, or crocheted piece produces a solid color unless two or more fibers were used in the cloth.

Cross-dyeing. Since not all fibers have the same affinity for dye, you can get interesting results by placing two or more fibers in the same dyebath and then spinning them into yarn.

Hints on Natural Dyeing

1. Wear rubber gloves. Dyes will stain your hands.
2. Pulverize or crush your dyestuff to bring out maximum dye pigments.
3. Save unused dyebaths by canning or freezing them.
4. Remember that wet yarn is darker than dry yarn.
5. Color will vary from bath to bath. Dye all yarn for one project in one bath.
6. Don't expose wool to sudden temperature changes. Rinse it gradually in successively cooler baths.
7. Avoid using metal containers, such as cast iron ones. They can affect the color of the dye. Enamel pots clean quite easily with a mild abrasive. Other metals tend to leave permanent stains.
8. Keep records for future reference (see page 45).
9. Remember that natural dyeing is largely a matter of experimentation. Enjoy it!

"Canyon Landscape" and "Arizona Poppies," tapestries by Ruth Friend. Hand-spun wool dyed in logwood chips, indigo, eucalyptus leaves, daffodils, onion skins, walnut leaves, and madder.

(Top row) Overdyeing: cochineal over white, blue, and yellow yarns. (Middle row) Yarns dyed in full-strength and diluted logwood dyebaths; a dip-dyed yarn; a tie-dyed yarn. (Bottom row) Cross-dyeing: a plied yarn mixture of different fibers dyed in the same dyebath (each accepted the indigo dye differently) and yarn produced by dyeing one fiber in a bath of several related colors; a heather yarn (related colors mixed by carding dyed fibers); and a variegated yarn.

(You can also place a cloth of two or more fibers in a bath of two or more dyes.) To dye fibers two or more colors, place the fibers into the first dye, slowly pour in a second dye, and then add more fibers. Don't stir the bath. Use colors that will blend well—for instance, blue and green, green and purple, red and orange. (Remember that complementary colors such as red and green tend to produce a muddy effect.) When using powdered synthetic dyes, sprinkle the dyes directly onto the fibers. Fill your container with water. Do not stir the contents. Remove the fiber carefully from the dyebath and squeeze while rinsing.

Diluting dyes. Diluting the dyebath produces lighter tones. A dye-bath that is almost exhausted also produces lighter tones.

Dip-dyeing. Dip a skein of yarn halfway into one color dyebath. Hold the skein until it is a shade darker than desired. Rinse clear. Hold the other end of the skein in a dyebath of another color. Colors may meet for a two-color yarn, or you can leave an undyed space between the dips for a three-color yarn.

Heather yarn. This yarn has flecks of related colors throughout. Prepare a heather by following the directions for cross-dyeing, or dye fibers separately and then mix into heather using card-ers. Choose related colors such as red, pink, and purple.

Mixing dyes. Dyes may be mixed to change colors. Follow the color rules. Complementary colors do not mix, except to produce brown.
Red and blue = purple
Red and yellow = orange
Blue and yellow = green
Adding black will produce a grayed effect.

Overdyeing. Dye one color over another to produce varying tones of the same hue or to change a color. Dye a darker color over a lighter one.

Tie-dyeing. Tie string or rubber bands around the skein at in-tervals. To dye more than one color, use an eyedropper to in-sert another color between yarns, then tie that area tightly and dip the entire skein into dyebath. You may dip the ends in another color and then tie them to preserve that color; then dip the entire piece in the dyebath. Remove ties after you rinse the yarn.

Variegated yarn. Dye fibers in various and separate dyebaths. Spin into yarn, alternating three to five colors as you spin.

RECORDS

Since natural dyeing is largely a matter of experimentation, don't expect to produce the exact shades shown on the color wheel. Don't even expect to always produce the same shade in the same dyebath. If you want to produce exactly the same shade for all of your yarns, immerse all of the yarn at once in the same dyebath. You will find that subsequent dyeing in the same bath will produce lighter and lighter tints, until the dye is exhausted.

Keep records and charts of your dyeing experiments similar to the one below. Attach a sample to the chart in your notebook. Don't trust your memory to do your recording!

DYEING EXPERIMENT

Dyeing done by _____ Date _____

Project dyed _____ Quantity _____

Dyestuff _____ Amount _____

Gathered: Date _____ Location _____

Mordant _____ Amount _____

Proportion of water to mordant _____

Proportion of water to dyestuff _____

Procedure:

Special techniques:

Sample:

Comments:

Three woven hangings by Norma Simmons. Natural gray wool, karakul, goat hair, and mohair.

Crocheted shawl of natural-colored wools worked in filet mesh technique, by Marilla Svinicki (owned by Jeri Pratt). Wool was spun on a Saxony Wheel.

Projects

The practical and aesthetic uses of homespun and dyed yarns are as varied as they are exciting. They range from weaving to rugmaking, from crocheting and knitting to macramé work. These projects are merely a suggestion of what you can begin to do with yarn you have spun and dyed yourself. Throughout the book you will find other examples of work by contemporary craftsmen; they are here not only to show you what can be accomplished but also to stimulate you to develop your own designs.

Weaving

Weavings can be made entirely of hand-spun yarns, or from a combination of hand-spun and commercial yarns. However, any yarn that is used for warp on a loom must be strong enough to hold up under tension. The stronger fibers such as silk, nylon, and linen make excellent warp in singles. Weaker fibers should be spun with a goodly amount of twist and plied before they are used to make a warp. To test a potential warp yarn, pull it apart with both hands. If it breaks easily, do not use it.

Almost any fiber can be used for the weft, depending upon the final purpose of the weaving. For instance, a strong weft should be used for an upholstery fabric that will receive a lot of wear. For a wall hanging, where strength is not important, even unspun fibers can be incorporated in the weaving.

Woven pillow cover by Winnie Ver Haagh. Hand-spun wool dyed in synthetic dyes, with stripes of unspun natural-colored wool added for texture.

RYA WALL HANGING

Rya is a lovely pile weave that can be worked on a loom as directed here, or knotted into a canvas or burlap backing. It consists of pieces of yarn that are folded in half and knotted around two warp ends. Approximately ¾ inch of plain weave is left between each row of knots. If you have a small loom, you can make the rya described here in smaller squares and then sew them together. To work the rya into burlap, pull out two rows of weft every ¾ inch and follow the instructions for knotting. The finished hanging is pictured on page 50.

Materials
3 pounds natural white wool
5 ounces wool fiber to be dyed
400 yards linen (flax) or cotton carpet warp
2 ounces each horse chestnuts, milkweed blossoms, marigold
  blossoms, black walnut hulls, onion skins
1 teaspoon iron sulphate
1½ ounces alum
driftwood (for hanging)

Directions for dyeing. Prepare the following dyebaths, referring to pages 39–42 for more specific directions on mordanting and dyeing.
Horse chestnuts. Use 2 ounces chestnuts to ½ teaspoon iron sulphate and ½ gallon water. Add 1 ounce wool fiber.
Milkweed blossoms. Use 2 ounces milkweed blossoms to ½ ounce alum and ½ gallon water. Add 1 ounce wool fiber.
Marigold blossoms. Use 2 ounces marigold blossoms to ½ ounce alum and ½ gallon water. Add 1 ounce wool fiber.
Walnut hulls. Use 2 ounces black walnut hulls to ½ teaspoon iron sulphate and ½ gallon water. Add 1 ounce wool fiber.
Onion skins. Use 2 ounces onion skins to ½ ounce alum and ½ gallon water. Add 1 ounce wool fiber.

Directions for spinning. Spin a medium-heavy single yarn from the 3 pounds of white wool, using the woolen method (see page 33). Spin a medium-heavy single yarn from each of the dyed fibers. Spin a warp from linen (without too much twist) or use a commercially prepared cotton or linen rug warp.

Directions for warping. These directions are for a two- or four-harness loom at least 20 inches wide. However, you can use a frame loom or a smaller harness loom if you make the hanging in small squares and piece them together afterwards.
Sett: 10 ends per inch
Total number of ends: 200
Width on loom: 20 inches
Length of warp: 2 yards

Rya wall hanging in natural-colored wool by Winnie Ver Haagh. Wool for the diamond design dyed in onion skins, horse chestnuts, milkweed blossoms, marigold blossoms, and black walnut hulls. (Instructions on page 49.)

Threading. Thread on a straight draw. Use a tabby or plain weave for the ¾ inch of filling between each row of knots.

Design. This is a simple design that does not really require a color sketch. You may work the diamond shape directly into the weaving or use a marker to draw an outline directly onto the stretched warp. You can also draw your design on brown paper and tape it to the back of the weaving.

Directions for weaving. You can make pile yarn in one of two ways: *Method 1:* Cut a piece of heavy cardboard, 4 × 2 inches. Wind the yarn around this gauge lengthwise and cut at one end. Cut all the dyed yarn and 2 pounds of the white wool. Use the remainder of the white wool for the weft. *Method 2:* Make butterflies of the yarn. Wrap the butterfly around the two warp ends, leaving a pile height of 2 inches. Cut the loop with a scissors after knotting.

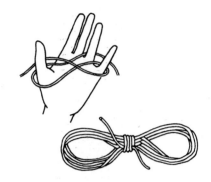

Making a butterfly

For hanging

1. Leave 10 inches of warp for the fringe before beginning to weave.

2. Using white woolen yarn, weave 2 inches of plain weave.

3. Every inch or so across, pick up one warp end with your fingers. Insert a 24-inch piece of driftwood.

4. Weave another 2 inches of plain weave.

5. Tie a row of rya knots. Work from left to right. Each knot is made with one piece of cut yarn or a butterfly. *Using cut yarn (method 1),* go down between two warp ends, under the left warp, up and over the left and right warp, under the right warp and up between the two warp ends. Pull the two ends forward and toward you. Repeat across. *Using the butterfly (method 2),* go down between two warp ends, under the left warp, up and over the left and right warp ends, leaving a 2-inch pile, then under the right warp and up between the two warp ends.

6. Weave a tabby weave with white woolen yarn for ¾ inch.

7. Repeat steps 5 and 6 until hanging is 25 inches, or desired length. Work diamond design into the piece, using all the dyed fibers, as you go.

8. Weave 2 inches of tabby with white woolen yarn. Insert driftwood as in step 3. Weave another 3 inches.

9. Remove weaving from loom.

10. Stitch a 3-inch heading to the back of the hanging. Insert another piece of driftwood for use as a hanging device.

11. Secure fringe by working an overhand knot over each group of eight warp ends.

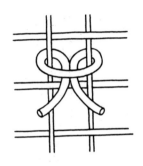

Finished rya knot

WOVEN TABLE RUNNER

This is a simple project which makes use of a two-ply wool warp and variegated weft. If you have been experimenting with small amounts of dyes and fibers, spinning a variegated yarn from them is a good way to make use of small quantities. The dyestuffs used in the directions given here are grass, onion skins, marigold blossoms, birch bark, and logwood chips. You can use a two-harness loom or you can fashion a loom from stretcher sticks or an old picture frame. The finished project is pictured on the facing page.

Materials
2½ ounces wool fiber to be dyed
3 ounces two-ply wool warp (approximately 150 yards)
¼ pound each grass, onion skins, marigolds, birch bark
2 ounces logwood chips
3 teaspoons iron sulphate
1 ounce blue vitriol
2 ounces alum

Directions for dyeing. Prepare the following dyebaths, referring to pages 39–42 for more specific directions on mordanting and dyeing.
Grass. Use ¼ pound grass to 1 gallon water and 1 ounce blue vitriol. Add ½ ounce wool fiber.
Onion skins. Use ¼ pound onion skins to 1 gallon water and 1 ounce alum. Add ½ ounce wool.
Marigolds. Use ¼ pound marigold blossoms to 1 gallon water and 1 ounce alum. Add ½ ounce wool.
Birch bark. Use ¼ pound birch bark to 1 gallon water and 1 teaspoon iron sulphate. Soak bark in water two to three days. Add ½ ounce wool.
Logwood chips. Soak 2 ounces logwood chips one or two days in a small amount of water. Use 2 ounces logwood chips to 1 gallon water and 2 teaspoons iron sulphate. Add ½ ounce wool fiber.

Directions for spinning. For the warp, use a long staple wool and spin a fine, strong, single yarn, using the worsted method (see page 33). Ply two single worsteds together for the warp.

For the weft, card wool into small rolags. Leave some noils or nubs for a textured effect. Spin one rolag of grass-dyed wool; attach onion skin-dyed wool and spin it. Attach the other colors at random, varying the length of each.

Repeat colors at random until the bobbin or the spindle is full. Wind yarn into balls. Yarn should be medium-weight and slightly nubby.

(Left) Woven table runner by Eunice Svinicki. Variegated wool yarn dyed in grass, onion skins, marigold blossoms, birch bark, and logwood chips. (Instructions on facing page.)

Tapestry of hand-spun wool dyed in natural dyes, by Glenna Gray. Fringe is strung with lead fishing weights.

Three-dimensional stuffed hanging by Norma Simmons. Wool dyed in eucalyptus leaves; copper wire binds the fringe.

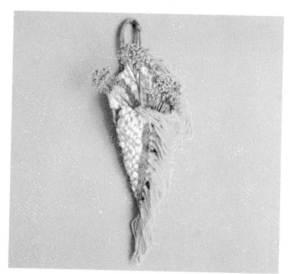

(Above) Woven weed holder by Mary Noonan, combining natural ram's wool and wool dyed in onion skins. (Right) Weed holder woven over cardboard loom, by Eunice Svinicki. (Instructions on facing page.)

Woven pillow covers by Eunice Svinicki. On the left, a sampler of hair fibers (horse, camel, wool, goat, dog, wolf, fox, mohair, and alpaca). Fur, partial knotting, and unspun fibers form the background weft for the middle pillow. Clippings from the author's three poodles were used for the yarn spun for the pillow on the right.

Directions for weaving
Sett: 10 ends per inch
Total number of ends: 100
Width on loom: 10 inches
Length of warp: 1½ yards

Threading. Thread on a straight draw.

Leave an allowance for fringe at onset of weave. Weave a tabby or plain weave with variegated yarn as the weft. Work to 20 inches. Remove from loom, leaving a 6-inch allowance for fringe.

For fringe, tie four warp ends each in an overhand knot. Trim to 4-inch lengths.

WOVEN WEED HOLDER

Work this project on a cardboard loom, using materials from your leftovers and experiments. You can fill the holder (see facing page) with weeds you have picked and dried yourself.

Materials
2 ounces assorted yarns
large-eyed needle
a piece of heavy cardboard, 9 × 12 inches

Directions for preparing warp and loom. Cut slits in each 12-inch end of a 9 × 12-inch piece of cardboard. Space slits ⅛ inch apart and approximately ¼ inch deep. Choose a medium to fine weight of yarn for the warp. (Note that the warp does not have to be strong on a cardboard loom.) Beginning at the left side, tie a knot in the end of your yarn and slip this knotted end into the first slit in the top of the cardboard. Bring yarn down to first slit at bottom of cardboard, over to second slit, back up to second slit at top, over to third slit and back to bottom third slit. Continue in this manner until cardboard is warped. Tie a knot to secure last slit.

Directions for weaving. Cut the yarn which is to be used for weft into 1-yard lengths and thread on a large-eyed needle. Starting at the bottom of cardboard, weave weft yarn across in a plain weave (over one warp and under one warp). Continue weaving in a plain weave, alternating colors for a striped effect. Beat each row firmly in place with a fork, comb, or your fingers. Be certain that the first and last rows are firmly beaten against the slits in the cardboard. Pop off weaving from cardboard. Fold weaving in half and sew up bottom and side seams. Turn to right side and line with a colorful fabric. Place your favorite dried weeds in the holder.

Knitting and Crocheting

If you are planning to knit or crochet garments out of your homespun yarn, use a soft, fairly consistent wool. (A tightly spun worsted would be scratchy and uncomfortable for wearing apparel; a consistent yarn is necessary to maintain proper gauges.) If you plan to make wall decorations, place mats, or rugs, you can choose from a much wider range of fibers and yarns.

KNITTED PILLOW COVER

This pillow cover (see page 59) uses the seed and popcorn stitches, and cabling. Try spinning the wool yarn for this project "in the grease." The cover may then be washed and later dyed.

Materials
9 ounces "in the grease" white wool
size 10½ knitting needles
double-pointed needle for cabling

Directions for spinning. Choose a medium-staple white wool which is quite clean and free from foreign matter. Tease and card the wool to free as much hay and chaff from it as possible. Do not wash the wool. Spin a medium-weight single yarn "in the grease." You will find that your fingers feel oily from the natural lanolin in the wool.

(Below) Knitted mittens of natural gray wool by Ruth Scherer. Yarn for the thumb and fingers was spun tightly to help reduce wear. (Below right) Knitted cape by Helene Svinicki, worked with extra-large needles and natural-colored wool.

Directions for knitting. Cast on 48 stitches with size 10½ knitting needles. Work in pattern as follows:

Row 1: k1, p1, 4 times; k6; k1, p1, 4 times; k4; k1, p1, 4 times; k6; k1, p1, 4 times.

Row 2: p1, k1, 4 times; p6; p1, k1, 4 times; p4; p1, k1, 4 times; p6; p1, k1, 4 times.

Row 3: k1, p1, 4 times; work a cable over next 6 stitches as follows: slip first 3 sts to a double-pointed needle, hold in back of work, k next 3 sts, k 3 sts from needle; k1, p1, 3 times; k1; slip next st on double-pointed needle, hold in back of work, k next 2 sts; p st from needle; slip next 2 sts onto needle, hold in front of work; p next st; k 2 sts from needle; p1; k1, p1, 3 times; cable over next 6 sts; k1, p1, 4 times.

Row 4: p1, k1, 4 times; p6; p1, k1, 3 times; p2; k1; p1; p2; k1; p1, k1, 3 times; p6; p1, k1, 4 times.

Row 5: k1, p1, 4 times; k6; k1, p1, 3 times; slip next st to needle and hold in back of work; k next 2 sts; p st from needle; p1; k1; slip next 2 sts to needle, hold in front of work; k next st; k2 from needle; k1, p1, 3 times; k6; k1, p1, 4 times.

Row 6: p1, k1, 4 times; p6; p1, k1, 3 times; p2; k1, p1, 2 times; p2; p1, k1, 3 times; p6; p1, k1, 4 times.

Row 7: k1, p1, 4 times; k6; k1, p1, 2 times; k1; slip next st to needle, hold in back of work; k next 2 sts; k st from needle; p1, k1, 2 times; slip next 2 sts to needle, hold in front of work; k next st; k 2 sts from needle; p1, k1, 2 times; p1; k6; k1, p1, 4 times.

Row 8: p1, k1, 4 times; p6, p1, k1, 2 times; p3; p1, k1, 3 times; p2; k1, p1, 2 times; k1; p6; p1, k1, 4 times.

Row 9: k1, p1, 4 times; work cable over next 6 sts; k1, p1, 2 times; slip next st to needle, hold in back of work; k next 2 sts; p st from needle; k1, p1, 3 times; slip next 2 sts to needle, hold in front of work; p next st; k 2 sts from needle; k1, p1, 2 times; cable over next 6 sts; k1, p1, 4 times.

Row 10: p1, k1, 4 times; p6; p1, k1, 2 times; p2; k1, p1, 4 times; p2; p1, k1, 2 times; p6; p1, k1, 4 times.

Row 11: k1, p1, 4 times; k6; k1; p1; k1; slip next st to needle, hold in back of work; k2; k st from needle; p1, k1, twice; cast on 2 sts; turn work around; p3 sts; turn work around; k3 sts; turn work around; p2 tog; p1; turn work around; k2 tog; p1, k1, twice; slip 2 sts to needle, hold in front of work; k next st; k2 from needle; p1; k1; p1; k6; k1, p1, 4 times.

Row 12: p1, k1, 4 times; p6; p1; k1; p4; k1, p1, 5 times; p1, k1, twice; p6; p1, k1, 4 times.

Row 13: k1, p1, 4 times; k6; k1; p1; slip next st to needle, hold in back of work; k2; p st from needle; k1, p1, 5 times; slip next 2 sts to needle, hold in front of work; k next st; k2 from needle; k1; p1; k6; k1, p1, 4 times.

Row 14: p1, k1, 4 times; p6; p1; k1; p2; k1, p1, 6 times; p2; p1; k1; p6; p1, k1, 4 times.

Row 15: k1, p1, 4 times; cable over next 6 sts; k1; p1; k2; p1, k1, 6 times; k2; k1; p1; cable over next 6 sts; k1, p1, 4 times.

Row 16: p1, k1, 4 times; p6; p1; k1; p2; k1, p1, 6 times; p2; p1; k1; p6; p1, k1, 4 times.

Row 17: k1, p1, 4 times; k6; k1; p1; slip next 2 sts to needle, hold in front of work; p1; k1 from needle; k1, p1, 5 times; slip next st to needle, hold in back of work; k2; p st from needle; k1; p1; k6; k1, p1, 4 times.

Row 18: p1, k1, 4 times; p6; p1; k1; p3; p1, k1, 5 times; p2; k1; p1; k1; p6; p1, k1, 4 times.

Row 19: k1, p1, 4 times; k6; k1; p1; k1; slip next 2 sts to needle, hold in front of work; k next st; k2 from needle; p1, k1 2 times; cast on 2 sts; turn work around; p3; turn work around; k3; turn work around; p2 tog; p1; turn work around; k2 tog; p1, k1, 2 times; slip next st to needle, hold in back of work; k2; k st from needle; p1; k1; p1; k6; k1, p1, 4 times.

Row 20: p1, k1, 4 times; p6; p1, k1 twice; p2; k1, p1, 4 times; p2; p1, k1, two times; p6; p1, k1, 4 times.

Row 21: k1, p1, 4 times; cable over next 6 sts; k1, p1, twice; slip next 2 sts to needle; k next st; k2 from needle; k1, p1, 3 times; slip next st to needle, hold in back of work; k2 sts from needle; p st from needle; k1, p1, twice; cable over next 6 sts; k1, p1, 4 times.

Row 22: p1, k1, 4 times; p6; p1, k1, twice; p3; p1, k1, 3 times; p2; k1, p1, twice; k1; p6; p1, k1, 4 times.

Row 23: k1, p1, 4 times; k6; k1, p1, twice; k1; slip next 2 sts to needle, hold in front of work; p next st; k2 sts from needle; p1, k1, twice; slip next st to needle, hold in back of work; k next 2 sts; p st from needle; p1, k1, twice; p1; k6; k1, p1, 4 times.

Row 24: p1, k1, 4 times; p6; p1, k1, 3 times; p2; k1, p1, twice; p2; p1, k1, 3 times; p6; p1, k1, 4 times.

Row 25: k1, p1, 4 times; k6; k1, p1, 3 times; slip next 2 sts to needle, hold in front of work; p next st; k2 sts from needle; k1; p1; slip next st to needle; hold in back of work; k2 sts; p st from needle; k1, p1, 3 times; k6; k1, p1, 4 times.

Row 26: p1, k1, 4 times; p6; p1, k1, 3 times; p4; k1; p2; k1, p1, 3 times; k1; p6; p1, k1, 4 times.

Row 27: k1, p1, 4 times; cable over next 6 sts; k1, p1, 3 times; k1; slip next 2 sts to needle, hold in front of work; p1 st; k2 from needle; slip next st to needle, hold in back of work; k2 sts; p st from needle; p1, k1, 3 times; p1; cable over next 6 sts; k1, p1, 4 times.

Row 28: p1, k1, 4 times; p6; p1, k1, 4 times; p4; p1, k1, 4 times; p6; p1, k1, 4 times.

Row 29: k1, p1, 4 times; k6; k1, p1, 4 times; slip next 2 sts to needle, hold in back of work; k2; k2 sts from needle; k1, p1, 4 times; k6; k1, p1, 4 times.

Repeat rows 2–29 twice more for pattern. On first repeat work cable over rows 5, 11, 17, 23, and 29. On last repeat work cable over rows 7, 13, 19, and 25. Bind off on row 29. Make another section. Stitch the two sections together. Wash in a mild soap bath until clean; rinse. Stuff to prevent shrinkage.

CROCHETED STOLE

Worked with a large crochet hook and mohair, this project, pictured on the facing page, takes little time. The simple cluster stitch is used throughout.

Materials
10 ounces mohair
size K crochet hook

Directions for spinning. Prepare a medium-fine weight of yarn from mohair. Wind the single yarn into balls.

Directions for crocheting. With size K crochet hook and a single strand of mohair yarn, ch 47 sts. Work all rows as follows: work 1 dc in 2nd ch from hook; *ch 1, skip 2 sts, work 2 dc in next ch; repeat from * 14 times; end ch 1, skip next 2 sts, work 1 dc in last ch, ch 1, turn work.
Repeat the above until 60 inches, or desired length, has been worked. Fasten off.

Fringe. Cut a 24-inch piece of yarn for fringe. Attach two doubled strands in every fourth stitch across each end of the stole. Finished fringe should be trimmed to 11 inches.

CROCHETED PLACE MAT

Hemp is an exciting fiber to spin. It works up into a coarse, natural-colored yarn suitable for place mats, hangings, and other decorative accessories. This place mat (see facing page) is worked in a simple filet mesh technique.

Materials
size J crochet hook
3 ounces hemp for each place mat

Directions for spinning. Spin a medium-fine weight of yarn, using 3 ounces of hemp for each place mat. For a smoother yarn, comb the fibers and dress a distaff as explained on page 20. Moisten your fingers while spinning. For a rougher, fuzzier yarn, use the fiber in carded form or as it comes from the supplier.

Directions for crocheting. With size J crochet hook, ch 27 sts.
Row 1: starting with 2nd ch from hook, sc in each ch; ch 1; turn.
Row 2: starting with 2nd st from hook *work 1 dc; ch 1; skip next st. Repeat from * across; end with 1 dc in last stitch; ch 2; turn. (Insert hook through both loops of each stitch in row 2.)
Repeat rows 1 and 2 twelve times, ending with row 1.
Finishing. Work a row of sc around the edge of the entire piece. Block to a uniform rectangle.

(Left) Crocheted stole of white mohair by Eunice Svinicki. (Instructions on facing page.)

(Above) Knitted pillow cover of natural-colored wool by Eunice Svinicki. (Instructions on page 56.)

(Above) Knitted mittens by Helene Svinicki. Natural-colored slub wool and indigo-dyed slub wool; yarn for cuffs dyed in sumac berries. (Left) Crocheted place mat of natural hemp, by Eunice Svinicki (see facing page).

(Above) Macramé hanging of natural-colored wool mounted on driftwood, by Eunice Svinicki. Driftwood was also used for the beads on the fringe. (Right) Macramé hanging of black wool (karakul), by Eunice Svinicki. Turkey neck bones are knotted onto the fringe. (Instructions on facing page.)

Macramé

Homespun and dyed yarns can add interesting textural and color effects to macramé projects. Since the yarn must be strong enough to hold up under constant manipulation, choose yarns that have a goodly amount of twist or are plied.

KARAKUL WALL HANGING (NAVAJO SPUN)

Since this hanging (see facing page) is made of very heavy yarn, use a Navajo spindle to spin the yarn. Turkey neck bones make unique beads for the fringe.

Materials
140 yards heavy black woolen yarn
18-inch piece of driftwood or dowel
turkey neck bones
7-inch embroidery hoop

Directions for spinning. Spin a heavy single yarn from black wool using a Navajo spindle (see pages 26–27). Spin 140 yards. The yarn should be ⅜ to ½ inch in diameter.

Directions for macramé
1. Cut yarn into fourteen pieces, each 10 yards long.
2. Use a larkshead knot to mount each doubled strand to driftwood. Wind the yarn into butterflies (28 single strands).
3. With each group of four strands, work 6 inches of half-knot sinnets, knotting the two outside strands over the center two strands. (You will have seven sinnets all together.)
4. Work two rows of horizontal double half hitches.
5. Work two rows of diagonal double half hitches over left half (13) strands.
6. Work two rows of diagonal double half hitches over other half of strands. Rows should meet in center to form a chevron.
7. Work 8 inches of alternating square knots.
8. Work one row of horizontal double half hitches.
9. Mount a 7-inch embroidery hoop into work: Leaving 3 inches of floating cords at top of hoop, use double half hitches to mount cords onto hoop. Three outer cords on each side should not be mounted to hoop. Before mounting cords to bottom half of hoop, divide cords in half and tie a loose half hitch in the middle of the hoop. Finish mounting cords at bottom half of hoop. Leave 3 inches of floating cords.
10. Work one row of horizontal double half hitches.

To finish. Cut off strands, leaving a 12-inch length for fringe. Tie turkey bones at random heights, using overhand knots.

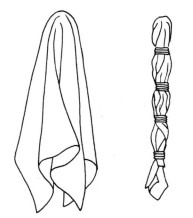

Bunch up scarf in center and tie into four sections.

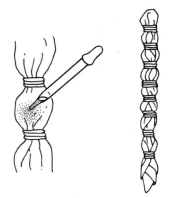

Drop dye between folds with eyedropper; tie off these dyed sections.

Dip center of scarf into dyebath; tie off dyed center.

Tie-dye and Batik

Although tie-dye and batik do not use yarns, you can certainly make use of natural dyeing in these textile crafts. Since synthetic fibers do not accept natural dyes very easily, natural fabrics are best. Sometimes, however, even natural fibers have chemical finishes on them which retard dyeing. Several washings may be necessary to remove these chemical finishes.

TIE-DYED SCARF

Designs are formed in tie-dyeing by banding areas of the fabric where you do not want dye to penetrate. This scarf is tied to form diamond shapes. Silk fabric, which readily accepts dye, was used for this scarf, pictured on the facing page.

Materials
square silk scarf
½ ounce cochineal
1 ounce logwood chips
1 ounce alum
1 teaspoon tin
rubber bands
eyedropper

Directions for preparing dye. Prepare the following dyebaths:
Cochineal. Use ½ ounce cochineal to 1 gallon water and 1 teaspoon tin.
Logwood chips. Use 1 ounce logwood chips to 2 quarts water.

Directions for mordanting. Add scarf to a solution of 1 ounce alum to 1 gallon water. Simmer for one hour.

Directions for tieing and dyeing. Find the center of your scarf. Bunch up the scarf from the center and tie off into four sections (see diagrams). Each tie should be about an inch wide. With an eyedropper, drop logwood dye into folds between each of these tied-off sections. Then band the logwood-dyed areas to maintain this color. Dip the center of the scarf into the logwood dyebath. Leave it in the dye for half an hour. Then tightly band this section, also. Now dye the entire scarf in the cochineal dyebath. Simmer for an hour. Rinse thoroughly, untie, and rinse again.

BATIK SCARF

Batik uses a wax-resist technique. The desired design is painted on in wax; when the fabric is dyed, the wax resists the dye. When you use natural dyes, the dyebath temperature must be less than the melting temperature of the wax; otherwise, the design will melt away in the hot dyebath. Use equal parts of paraffin and beeswax; if you wish to obtain more "veins," use 2 parts paraffin to 1 part beeswax. The designs that are possible in batik are as infinite as your imagination.

Materials
square silk scarf
paraffin and beeswax
watercolor brushes
2 ounces madder
¼ ounce each tin and chrome
¼ ounce iron sulphate
½ pound black walnut hulls
stretcher sticks the size of the scarf
¼ ounce iron sulphate
thumbtacks
newspaper
candy thermometer

Directions for waxing and dyeing
1. Prepare a dyebath from 2 ounces of madder to 1 gallon water and ¼ ounce each of tin and chrome. Dye the entire scarf in this bath, allowing it to simmer for approximately one hour. Rinse thoroughly.
2. Stretch the wet scarf over stretcher sticks or an old picture frame. Secure with thumbtacks.
3. Heat wax in a double boiler, bringing wax to 150–200° F. reading on candy thermometer. With watercolor brushes, paint the outline and center of daisylike flowers (do not fill in petal shapes). Paint at random over entire scarf. Then paint entire background or spaces in between the flower outlines with wax so that only the daisy petal shapes are not waxed.
4. Remove scarf from sticks and crumple it to crack the wax.
5. Prepare a dyebath from black walnut hulls. Use ½ pound of hulls to 1 gallon water and ¼ ounce iron sulphate. Soak the waxed scarf in this dyebath overnight. (Leave the bath at room temperature to avoid overheating.)
6. Rinse scarf until water runs clear.
7. Press scarf between layers of newspaper until all wax is removed. Change papers frequently.

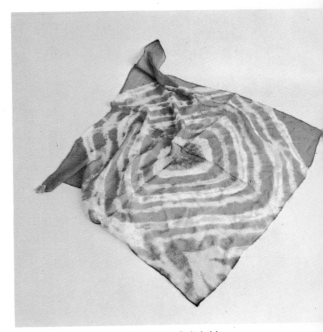

Tie-dyed scarf by Eunice Svinicki, dyed in cochineal and logwood chips (see facing page).

Batik silk scarf by Eunice Svinicki, dyed in madder and black walnut hulls.

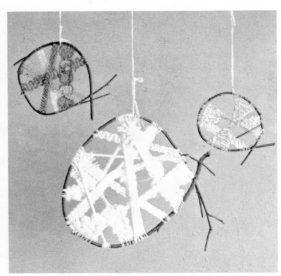

Weavings done over twigs, by Winnie Ver Haagh.

Bibliography

Adrosko, Rita J., *Natural Dyes and Home Dyeing.* U.S. Government Publications Reprint of *Natural Dyes in the U.S.,* 1968; also Dover Publications, New York, New York, 1971.

Anderson, Beryl, *Creative Spinning, Weaving and Plant Dyeing.* Arco Publishing Company, Inc., New York, New York, 1971.

Brooklyn Botanical Gardens, *Dye Plants and Dyeing, A Handbook.* Brooklyn, New York. 1973.

Davenport, Elsie G., *Your Handspinning.* Select Books, Pacific Grove, California, 1964.

Fannin, Allen, *Handspinning: Art and Technique.* Van Nostrand Reinhold Co., New York, New York, 1970.

Hight, Dee, *Innovative Spinning, Penguin Quill.* Hight Enterprises, Ltd., Boulder, Colorado, 1973.

Kluger, Marilyn, *The Joy of Spinning.* Simon and Schuster, New York, New York, 1971.

Lesch, Alma, *Vegetable Dyeing: One Hundred Fifty-One Recipes for Dyeing Yarn and Fabrics with Natural Materials.* Watson-Guptill, Inc., Cincinnati, Ohio, 1971.

Thurstan, Voiletta, *The Use of Vegetable Dyes.* The Dryad Press, Wood Ridge, New Jersey, 1972.

Tidball, Harriet, *Color and Dyeing.* Craft and Hobby Book Service, Select Books, Pacific Grove, California, 1965.

Ulster Museum, *Spinning Wheels.* Publication No. 168, The Ulster Museum, Belfast, Ireland, 1969.

Suppliers

The following suppliers carry basic spinning equipment, fibers, natural dyes, and mordants. All sell both retail and mail order.

Ashford Handicrafts, LTD.
P.O. Box 12
Rakaia
Canterbury, New Zealand
(also carries a spinning
   wheel kit)

Black Sheep Weaving &
   Craft Supply
318 S.W. 2nd St.
Corvallis, Ore. 97330

Clemes and Clemes
   Spinning Wheels
665 San Pablo Ave.
Pinole, Calif. 94564
(also supplies and repairs
   parts for wheels)

Greentree Ranch Wools
Countryside Handweavers
163 N. Carter Lake Rd.
Loveland, Colo. 80537

Halcyon
1121 California St.
Denver, Colo. 80202

Handcraft Wools
Box 378, Streetsville
Ontario, Canada

The Niddy Noddy
416 Albany Post Rd.
Croton-on-Hudson, N.Y.
   10520

Northwest Handcraft
   House
110 W. Esplanade
North Vancouver, B.C.
Canada

Riley St. Annex
630 5th St.
Santa Rosa, Calif. 95404

School Products Co., Inc.
1201 Broadway
New York, N.Y. 10001

The Sheep Village
2005 Bridgeway
Sausalito, Calif. 94965

The Spinster
34 Hamilton Ave.
Sloatsburg, N.Y. 10974

Straw Into Gold
P.O. Box 2904
5550 College Ave.
Oakland, Calif. 94618

The Weaving Depot
2701 Sepulveda Blvd.
Manhattan Beach, Calif.
   90266

The Yarn Depot, Inc.
545 Sutter St.
San Francisco, Calif.
   94102